LIVING
with
SHEEP

EVERYTHING YOU NEED TO KNOW
TO RAISE YOUR OWN FLOCK

❋

by Chuck Wooster

Photographs by Geoff Hansen

❋

The Lyons Press
Guilford, Connecticut
AN IMPRINT OF THE GLOBE PEQUOT PRESS

The Lyons Press is an imprint of The Globe Pequot Press

10 9 8 7 6 5 4 3 2 1

Printed in China
Designed by LeAnna Weller Smith

Library of Congress Cataloging-in-Publication Data

Wooster, Chuck.
   Living with sheep : everything you need to know to raise your own flock / by Chuck
Wooster ; photographs by Geoff Hansen.
      p. cm.
   ISBN 1-59228-531-7 (trade cloth)
Sheep. I. Title.

SF375.W86 2005
636.3—dc22

2004065025

For Sue, who took the plunge with me.

CONTENTS

Opposite: A Suffolk lamb contentedly munches on pasture grass at Harlow Brook Farm in Hartland, Vermont.

ACKNOWLEDGMENTS

Thanks to Geoff Hansen for launching this project and to Ann Treistman at The Lyons Press for bringing it home safely.

Thanks to Steve Long and Mary Hays for recognizing a shepherd in the making, answering the phone even when they knew it was me, reviewing this manuscript along the way, and showing me how to live with sheep. Additional thanks to Stan and Lucy Yarian for improving the final draft.

And thanks to everyone who turns up at Sunrise Farm just when an extra set of hands is needed: Bruce, Beckley, Jim, and Betsy Wooster; Heather Woodcock, Dan, Silas, and Louisa Monahan; Rachael Cohen; Carl Demrow; Steve Fulton; Kevin Comeau (on the home team); and, most of all, Sue Kirincich, who dashed out of the shower to help with the first birth.

—Chuck Wooster

Thanks to the sheep farmers who were generous with their time and their flocks: Linda and Tuthill Doane of Braintree, VT; John Lenihan of Strafford, VT; Barbara and Bob Mathewson of Plainfield, NH; Jennifer Megyesi and Kyle Jones of Royalton, VT; Sarah Taylor and Matt Dunne of Hartland, VT; John O'Brien of Tunbridge, VT; Steve Wetmore of Strafford, VT; and Marian White of Tunbridge, VT. And thanks to butchers Tom Eaton and Clint Hill of West Fairlee, VT, shearer Andy Rice of Halifax, VT, and the curious kids whom I met at the Tunbridge World's Fair. To Chuck Wooster, for his unwavering enthusiasm and diligence in writing this book. To editor Ann Treistman, for whom I owe many thanks for her ongoing support and thoughtfulness.

—Geoff Hansen

INTRODUCTION

Why Sheep?

Why sheep? Because sheep are soft and fuzzy and big enough to be challenging—yet not so big they can kill you with a kick or a butt. Because sheep have lambs. Because sheep are easy companions who require little beyond understanding. Because the wool sheep produce in abundance can be used for everything from sweaters to comforters to felt slippers to home insulation. Because a leg of lamb stuffed with garlic and rosemary and slowly roasted in your kitchen on a winter's afternoon will bring you to the apex of culinary achievement. And because, finally, as you sit in the hay on a spring morning with a warm, dry lamb sleeping in your arms and a watchful ewe breathing in your ear and nickering in the back of her throat to comfort the little fellow, you'll realize that you've grown unwilling to live without sheep. As my wife Sue once said as we walked into the barn and found our lambs asleep in a pile in the sunlight and the ewes chewing their cuds, with their eyes half-closed and their long ears swept back against their heads in a sign of pure contentment, "Wow. This is when you know that all is right with the world."

Opposite: Students Eben Holbrook, age ten, and Emma Kimball, nine, feed hay to one of the ewes in the sheep barn at the Tunbridge World's Fair in Tunbridge, Vermont. Kids from area schools attend the first day of the fair to see the animals.

There are lots of sheep books out there, and as you delve further into the details of raising sheep, you'll probably want to own several. But what I discovered as a person who had grown up in the suburbs—without the benefit of 4-H, farming neighbors, or hands-on agricultural experience of any kind—was that I knew too little to even understand many of the books.

 Above: Marian White's passion for sheep is reflected on the license plate of her motorcycle.

One book, for example, beautifully described a hundred and one ways in which lambs could be stuck inside a ewe and require assistance during birth. That was all well and good (OK, it was good and terrifying), but my questions were more fundamental: "What is normal lambing like? What is a typical birth?"

Another book listed the diseases and maladies of sheep in exhaustive detail. It's a list I have

since come to respect and appreciate, but that list didn't help me back when my questions were more basic: "What is a healthy sheep? How can I tell if mine are healthy?"

These are the questions that this book sets out to answer: the big-picture questions, the general cases, the wide range of options. As you get further into being a shepherd, you may gravitate toward certain aspects of shepherding, such as breeding, working with wool, or perhaps pasture improvement. That's when you may want to consult the references at the back of this book to find out which book to buy next.

I was extraordinarily fortunate to have purchased my flock from friends who live not far away. I was able to pepper them with all kinds of basic and embarrassingly naïve questions about living with sheep, and they calmly and steadily answered all of them—never once striking the mortal blow that I dreaded, "Where the heck did you grow up anyway, the suburbs?" I went to them with a photocopied list of everything one book said I'd need to buy before lambing season, a list that struck me as recommending more equipment than most third world medical clinics have. My friends put stars next to the half-dozen key items on the list and told me to forget about the rest. Ah, perspective! Relief! That's what this book is about.

Living with sheep doesn't have to be any more complicated or esoteric than living with cats or living with dogs. You learn the basics, you get to know your animals, and you call the vet (or a friend) if something difficult comes down the pike that you've never dealt with before.

I should warn you, however, that as a budding shepherd, you will encounter one great nuisance that comes with raising sheep, and that is this: every friend and acquaintance who comes to visit you and your flock will, sooner or later (and most likely sooner), ask something to the effect of, "Aren't sheep the stupidest animals in the barnyard?" "Aren't they dumber than posts, dumber than the fence that holds them in?"

Sheep are in a tough spot when seen through our eyes. They are large and fuzzy and give birth to cute offspring, and as such, we naturally lump them together with the other fuzzy mammals in our lives: cats and dogs. Yet cats and dogs are, like us, predators at heart, with eyes set close together and a brain designed to sense opportunity and play the angle. It's no wonder we delight in how smart Fido and Fifi are—they look at the world the same way we do.

Sheep do not. They are herbivores with eyes set widely apart because they are, fundamentally, a prey species—and a singularly unarmed one at that. Sheep have neither spikes on their tails nor thick armor on their backs. Their mouths lack canines or incisors on the upper palate. Though they can easily outpace the shepherd in the barnyard, their speed is nowhere near that of moose or deer, their wild cousins.

The great strategy that sheep have evolved in their defense is to stick together—and they will go to extraordinary measures to do so, even if it means charging through electric fencing or grazing cheek by jowl in a crowded corner of a large, otherwise empty pasture. When one sheep decides to leave the barn, suddenly they are all up and running, moving as one big, apparently stupid herd with no room for individual expression.

But step into the pasture and try to herd them through a gate, and your impression of sheep will change from brainless beasts to brilliant tacticians. Ramona, our oldest and wisest sheep, could maneuver any chess grand master into a corner. When I have a few spare minutes on my hands, I enjoy playing a match or two against her and her colleagues. I, moving slowly and nonchalantly, take a step to the left to cut off her angle away from the gate. She, her ears flapping gently against the summer's flies and apparently grazing without a care in the world, steps to the right. I think I have the herd trapped into a narrowing chute of fencing and she—somehow directing the whole flock—works them back into the open. It's a slow motion game of chess in which we both pretend not to be playing, and I always lose.

But sheep aren't the only barnyard animals that are, by nature, prey animals; cows and horses are equally wide-eyed in the face of hungry predators. Unlike sheep, however, cows and horses are large animals—far larger than coyotes, wolves, or mountain lions. This hasn't made them immune from hungry jaws, but it has provided them with a sense of perspective and the ability to stand fast and intimidate potential predators with their bulk and, if needed, a well-placed kick.

Sheep have these same abilities but on a much smaller scale. When our neighbor's tiny Shih Tzu dog slips through the fence to visit the sheep, Desdemona, our freckle-nosed captain of the guard, invariably moves toward the little fellow, swinging her head menacingly and stomping her hooves in challenge. This is just as effective against the little pup as it is for a stallion facing, say, a lone wolf or a handler wielding an unwelcome bridle.

But Desi immediately melts back into the flock if I step into the sheep pen unexpectedly, perhaps holding a needle dripping with vaccine. I am much larger than the dog and hence more of a potential threat. Yet I am a known quantity with a reasonable, if somewhat checkered, reputation in their eyes. With my vaccination needle poised, the flock adopts an "intermediate risk" strategy, their keep-away-from-the-shepherd tactic. It's amazing how a dozen reasonably large animals can squeeze through your fingers as easily as Jell-O if they're so inclined.

But if you, for example, were to step unexpectedly into our sheep pen holding the needle—a completely unknown commodity confronting them in an enclosed space—they would adopt the strategy for which they are most pilloried by human beings: the huddle.

In the huddle, the whole flock runs into a corner and jams their heads as far out of sight as possible. This appears to be a version of the if-I-can't-see-you-you-can't-see-me attitude displayed by human babies and simpletons. What better example of sheep stupidity is there?

I confess I shared this opinion until I happened to be sitting down in the pen with the sheep when an unexpected visitor caused the sheep to

Above: A Dorset Finn Southdown ewe rests with her 2½-week-old lambs—a ram at left and a ewe—in the warm barn at Fat Rooster Farm in Royalton, Vermont.

huddle up in the corner near me. With my eyes near ground level—and very near the level of a wolf's or coyote's eyes—the effect was startling. A dozen individual animals suddenly morphed into a great, twenty-four legged, wooly blob with no front, no back, no eyes, and no obvious place to gain a toehold—or a canine tooth-hold. If I had been a coyote on patrol, I would have thought seriously about going home for reinforcements before attempting to dismember such a large and weird-looking creature.

But back to the original question: Why sheep? In a profound sort of way, sheep are a lot like us. They are warm-blooded, they weigh about the same as we do, they give birth to cute offspring, they are obsessed with food, and they are inherently social creatures. The fact that their society is arranged differently from our society doesn't make them uninteresting; it makes them fascinating, and even exotic—like travel in foreign lands. Living with sheep will certainly get you outside into the sun, fresh air, and honest sweat of rural life. In the end, however, it will also show you a surprising amount about yourself and about those more familiar, warm-blooded mammals we all live with every day: our fellow human beings.

LIVING
~ with ~
SHEEP

CHAPTER ONE

Things to Think About in Advance

Let me confess at the outset that I didn't think much about the details of living with sheep until I got a flock of my own. Friends of mine were looking to sell their flock, my wife and I had just moved to an old farm, I had a vague notion about wanting to raise animals... sold!

This approach, of course, had the advantage of requiring very little thought or advance planning on my part. Before I knew what was going on, I was in over my head and encountering adventure and intrigue around every corner. If this sounds like your approach to life, then I say, "Go for it!"

But if your personality leans more toward the contemplative and deliberate—which mine usually does, or at least used to before I got involved in the sheep racket—allow me to offer some words of advice at the outset.

THREE APPROACHES TO LIVING WITH SHEEP

There are three general approaches to living with sheep. In order of increasing complexity, they are:

- **Keep it simple.** Buy lambs in the spring and raise them for the summer.
- **Glorified lawn mower.** Run sheep year-round to improve the view, keep your fields open, and add a certain pastoral aesthetic to your spread without delving into the details of breeding.

Opposite: Maddie, an Oxford cross ewe, looks into the barnyard. Owner Barbara Mathewson borrowed an Oxford ram from a friend one year for breeding her ewes. "I look for temperament more than breed for ease of lambing."

- **Fully fleeced.** Keep your own ewes, rams, and, therefore, lambs, throughout the year. In short, own a genuine flock.

The good news is that you can change your approach from year to year as your time and enthusiasm wax and wane. The bad news (or perhaps this is the good news) is that being "fully fleeced" requires the greatest effort but affords by far the greatest rewards.

Lambs for the Summer

Keeping it simple by buying lambs in the spring, raising them on grass for the summer, and slaughtering them in the fall is by far the best place to start if you're getting into shepherding for the first time and you aren't sure if you want to jump into the deep end right away.

For one, you get to watch lambs gamboling around your property all summer—jumping over logs, playing king of the mountain on any scrap of topography your pastures provide, and doing their four-footed, instantaneous vertical leaping called *stotting*. (The word *stotting* fails to capture the magic and hilarity of this behavior, but a better word, it seems, is still in the offing.)

Then there is the pleasant fact that you won't have to load your barn full of hay every summer, or indeed need a barn at all. Your expenses will be low. Your annual January vacation in the tropics will not be canceled. And finally, instead of trudging off to the barn on winter evenings at twenty below to feed your sheep, you'll be sitting in front of the fire and tucking into a hot bowl of lamb stew.

Keeping Adults Year-Round

But keeping lambs only in the summer has two distinct disadvantages. First, you never really get the chance to know your sheep; just when your lambs are starting to develop distinct personalities, off they go. (They "matriculate," as one of my friends says.) Second, there is something intensely profound about trundling out to the barn on that twenty below evening and finding your sheep peering out from within their thickest winter coats and giving

you the exceedingly convincing impression that they couldn't care less. It's an extraordinary sight: they'll have frost on their noses, ice on their backs, and a studied attitude of complete indifference. The simplicity of winter is one of the best times to enjoy living with sheep.

Keeping a flock year-round, therefore, will enable you to experience these twin

 Above: A Suffolk lamb scampers across the pasture at Harlow Brook Farm. Matt Dunne and Sarah Taylor buy the lambs from a local farm in May and butcher them in October. "We're raising our own food," Taylor said. "We know exactly where it came from."

 **Above:** A sign for wool hangs on Steve Wetmore's barn in Strafford, Vermont.

delights of personality and seasonality. Plus, you won't have to mow the lawn very often in the summer, and you'll be able to shear your sheep and either sell the wool or take up one of the many handicrafts using wool, such as knitting, weaving, spinning, or felting.

A BREEDING FLOCK

Of course, you can have it all—the stotting lambs, the wool, the meat, the friendships, and the frozen water troughs of January—which involves the most work but the most reward. After all, if you're going to keep sheep year-round anyway, and you've already put up the fencing and the shelter, why not just go for it? Keeping sheep without having them lamb may be simpler, but it's also more expensive; you don't have much revenue to put against all those expenses.

I confess that "fully fleeced" is how I got into the sheep business: from nothing to bona fide shepherd in the very few minutes it took to get out the checkbook. The key for me—and I'd strongly recommend it as the key for you too—is to buy your flock from someone you know and like (and vice versa). The friends from whom I bought my flock were available by phone whenever I needed them and were even willing to come by on the few occasions when I found myself deep in the weeds. They were able to point out at a glance that my hay feeder was too high for the sheep to reach and that Rachel's habit of ramming the other ewes with her head was perfectly normal. She was doing me the favor of keeping the rebels in line.

Regardless of which approach you decide to take, my strongest piece of advice is to buy your sheep from a friend or neighbor whom you know and trust. Reading books is great—especially, and hopefully, this book. But book learning will only get you so far, and there is no substitute for having an experienced eye look things over from time to time and help you sort out the worrisome from the normal. Someday soon, you too will have the experienced eye—and there's no finer feeling. But in the meantime, make sure you have someone nearby who can pilot you through the reefs and shoals.

Since owning a breeding flock year-round encompasses all of the details of the other two approaches, I'll assume throughout this book that you, too, have been "fully fleeced." If you decide to go for either the "keep it simple" or the "glorified lawn mower" route, you can simply ignore the sections that don't pertain to your operation.

THREE PIECES OF BIG-PICTURE ADVICE

With the three different approaches to living with sheep covered, here are three pieces of big-picture advice for the beginning shepherd—the three things I wish I'd known at the outset.

GET TO KNOW YOUR SHEEP

I was surprised to discover that my sheep are constantly communicating with one another and attempting to communicate with me. What are they saying? The sooner you can learn to understand sheep-speak, the easier your life will be. Some clues are obvious: when you see a reclining sheep with eyes half-closed, ears swept back, and a good wad of cud going in the

mouth, you know that you're doing everything just right.

But other clues are more obscure, and this is where it helps to know the distinct personalities of your individual sheep. Desdemona, the captain-of-the-guard sheep I mentioned in the introduction, is normally very reticent around me. She is among the last to approach the hay feeder and will try to keep at least one other animal between herself and me at all times. So I was surprised one day to find her standing close to the gate as I approached. She didn't move away from me as I worked in the pen, and she even came walking toward me at one point as I

 Above: Lily, a Romney ewe, casts a wary eye upon the photographer in Plainfield, New Hampshire. Owner Barbara Mathewson has had a small flock of sheep year-round since 1980.

Things to Think About in Advance **7**

was bending over to pick up some lumber that I had dropped. That's when I noticed she was hobbling on three legs, having cracked a hoof out on the pasture somewhere. Aha! I grabbed the hoof trimmers, clipped off the cracked nail, and off she went to rejoin the flock.

When it comes to making noise, sheep rarely "baa" unless they have good reason to. If your flock starts making a bunch of noise on an otherwise quiet afternoon, it's worth figuring out why. As you get to know them and they get to know you, you'll soon discover that you can tell at a glance when something is amiss and take steps to correct it before problems develop.

Have Your Sheep Get to Know You

The flip side, of course, is to let your sheep get comfortable with you. Sheep are creatures of routine, and recent research has shown that sheep can remember individual human faces for years between meetings. Sheep are more relaxed around someone they know, which makes it easier for you to get close to them and keep track of how they are doing. At times in the summer, I'll go so far as to sit down in the pasture or even take a nap while the flock grazes nearby. (Not when there's a ram in the pasture, however!) In the spring, I've set up a chair in the paddock and read a magazine while the ewes and lambs take turns coming over for a look. All of this helps the sheep become convinced that, while I'm still an unpredictable predator with scary eyes, I'm at least temporarily on their team.

Of the eight ewes that have been living with us for the past few years, Luna and Noche—two animals that were born on our farm and have lived with us ever since—are the friendliest with me. Almost all of the ewes will come up to me and say hi if I'm doing something inside their pen; but Luna and Noche will loiter right next to me even if I stumble into them by mistake. They seem far more comfortable with me than the other ewes born on other farms.

Aim for Stress-Free Living

Finally, your ultimate goal as a shepherd is for you and your sheep to live stress-free lives. Here are a few ways to help make that happen:

- **Maintain a routine.** Feed your sheep on a regular schedule so that they don't have to worry about when the next meal is coming.
- **Avoid chasing them around.** If you need to catch one, confine them all in a small area where they are easy to grab.
- **Don't make direct eye contact.** If you're walking among your sheep, don't make direct eye contact; they are hard-wired to interpret this as threatening.
- **Avoid any sudden movement.** Sudden movement can startle your sheep.
- **Talk to your sheep whenever you are working with them.** Talking to your sheep might cause your family and friends to think you are a bit crazy, but your calm, relaxed voice will soothe them in times of stress and worry. Over and over, I've seen my flock jump to attention as I approach them from far across a pasture only to see them relax and return to grazing as soon as they hear my customary "Hi girls!" greeting. The coast is clear—it's just him again. Nothing to worry about.

OK, that's it for big-picture advice. Now to the nitty gritty!

CHAPTER TWO

Choosing a Flock

Stories are often told in Vermont about the new-comer who moves to the country to experience the joys and delights of rural living. In one such tale, the hero has purchased a tractor, a chainsaw, several how-to books describing the intricacies of heating the house with wood, and he has immersed himself in the relative advantages of hard maple versus soft maple, oak versus beech, and white birch versus yellow birch. One day, dressed in crisp new woolens, our hero stops by the farm next door to strike up a conversation with his neighbor. "In your opinion," he asks, "what is the best firewood for heating your house in the winter?"

To which the farmer inevitably replies, "The stuff that's stacked closest to the woodstove."

This also happens to be good advice when starting out in the sheep business: choose a breed that is being raised nearby. If you buy your flock from a trusted friend or neighbor, he or she will be quick to offer advice and help you succeed. Plus, if you already trust that friend or neighbor, chances are good that he or she has already made a smart decision about which breed is best for your area. Choosing some exotic breed from far away will saddle you with a host of unnecessary logistical concerns.

Once you've become a master shepherd, you can always switch breeds if you discover there's another breed that's more to your liking. There are dozens of distinct and registered breeds out there, some of which feature hair, wool, colored faces, colored fleeces, no

Opposite: Michael the guard horse keeps an eye on a photographer overhead at Fat Rooster Farm. A retired national champion riding horse, the Anglo-Arabian keeps predators away from the sheep.

color, horns, hairless tails, or some combination of the above. There are purebreds, crossbreeds, heirloom breeds, breeds just introduced to the marketplace, and breeds that are just plain mutts. Don't be too hung up on your initial choice. As I said, you can always change your mind down the road by selling off your current flock or breeding your existing ewes to rams from your newly preferred breed.

If you live in an area that's teeming with sheep, however, you may have to choose between several friends and neighbors— each of whom is promoting the virtues of their preferred breed. Before you go knocking on doors, take a moment to consider what you ultimately want to do with your sheep. Do you plan to raise them for meat? For wool? For milk and cheese? For fun? For their historical value? Just for the heck of it? Your answers to these questions will guide you in selecting the right breed from among the choices in your neighborhood.

Shepherds are a jovial lot, and I have yet to meet anyone in the sheep biz who is anything less than pleasant and helpful. But there is one topic of conversation that is guaranteed to provoke a fistfight, even among this most mild-mannered of crowds: claiming that some other breed of sheep is better than theirs. Everyone, it seems, is a partisan. Rather than risk my good standing in the shepherd community by stating a preference, I'm simply going to divide the most common breeds up into one of four categories: the meat breeds, the wool breeds, the heirloom breeds, and the dairy breeds. My

goal is to help you choose a breed that works for you without unduly slandering one of the many dozens of breeds that may not suit your needs.

IMPROVED BREEDS: MEAT OR WOOL

If you think you want to raise sheep primarily or exclusively for their meat or their wool, you ought to focus on one of the many so-called "improved" breeds of sheep. These breeds have been carefully selected by shepherds over the years to be optimally

 Above: Steve Wetmore's Katahdin flock grazes near his stacked firewood. Wetmore uses his Katahdin flock—a breed that grows fur instead of wool—to train the Border collies he breeds and sells to other farms.

meaty or optimally wooly. This can make a big difference. Lambs from a meaty breed can grow twice as fast as those from a nonmeaty breed, which is an important consideration when you're selling meat by the pound. The same goes for wool: the fiber from wooly breeds can fetch more than ten times the price of that from nonwooly breeds. In fact, the wool from some nonwooly breeds can be worth almost nothing on the wool market.

Although I'm going to divide the meat and wool breeds into first-tier and second-tier lists, this refers to their history and genetic potential rather than to the price you should expect to pay to buy one. A healthy, happy, and well-formed animal from any breed is going to command top dollar, while a lesser specimen from any breed will not—even if I included that breed in the top tier. There are a few notes at the end of this chapter on what to look for when buying individual animals.

THE MEAT BREEDS

Sheep that have been bred for optimal meat production tend to be large, with dark faces and possibly colored wool (since they haven't been bred to have exclusively white wool), and be descendents of the famous British Isles meat breeds: Hampshire and Suffolk. Their top-tier membership roster includes:

Columbia	Hampshire	Suffolk
East Friesian	Oxford	

Second-tier meat breeds—breeds that produce good quantities of meat but aren't quite in the league with the superstars of the first list—include:

Border Leicester	Montadale	Southdown
Bluefaced Leicester	North Country	Targhee
Cheviot	Cheviot	Texel
Dorper	Polypay	Tunis
Dorset	Romney	Wiltshire
Katahdin	Rambouillet	Panama
Lincoln	Shropshire	

THE WOOL BREEDS

Sheep that have been bred for their wool production tend to be smaller, white-faced, white-wooled (since white wool can be more consistently dyed than naturally colored wool), and at least distantly related to that grand-champion southern European wool breed: the Merino. Wool breeds tend

Above: A Southdown cross ram lamb watches a visitor walk to the barn at Fat Rooster Farm. Owners Jennifer Megyesi and Kyle Jones raise over a hundred lambs each spring for their organic meat operation.

to have lost the coarse, outer coat of their wild ancestors in exchange for more of the soft, insulating inner coat that is so good for spinning and working. The star cast of wooly characters features:

American Cormo	Debouillet	Rambouillet
Booroola Merino	Delaine Merino	Targhee
Columbia	East Friesian	
Corriedale	Panama	

The second-tier wool breeds include:

Bluefaced Leicester	Montadale	Romney
Border Leicester	North Country Cheviot	Shropshire
Cheviot		Southdown
Clun Forest	Perendale	Texel
Dorset	Polypay	
Lincoln	Romeldale	

THE ALL-AROUND PUREBREDS

The observant among you will have noticed that several breeds show up on both the meat and the wool lists. In particular, the Columbia is a top performer in both categories—being originally a cross of the Rambouillet and Lincoln, each of which scores well in its respective category. The East Friesian also appears atop both categories and is also considered to be the best all-around milk-producing breed. Other all-around breeds that are favored for both meat and wool are the Border Leicester, Cheviot, Dorset, Lincoln, Montadale, North Country Cheviot, Lincoln, Polypay, Romney, Rambouillet, Shropshire, Southdown, and Targhee.

The even more observant among you will have noticed that I left the Bluefaced Leicester out of this list, even though it appears in both categories. Rather than being a general-purpose breed, the Bluefaced Leicester is used primarily to produce ewe lambs for sale to shepherds who will use them for crossbreeding (more on that in a minute). The Wensleydale is another such breed, while most of the all-star meat breeds—the Hampshire, Oxford, and Suffolk, along with the Shropshire, Southdown, and Texel—are used primarily to produce ram lambs for crossbreeding. In other words, shepherds who have purebred flocks of these breeds are raising them primarily for breeding stock, not for meat or wool.

UNIMPROVED, RARE, OR HEIRLOOM BREEDS

Don't forget the important subset of purebreds: the so-called unimproved, antique, or heirloom breeds. The very act of "improving" a breed for meat or wool means the inadvertent "de-proving" of some other trait—usually one related to heartiness and ease of lambing.

Opposite: Razzamatazz, a Shetland ewe lamb, looks around the pasture at Maple Ridge Sheep Farm in Braintree, Vermont. Owners Linda and Tuthill Doane imported the first Shetlands into the United States in 1986.

Heirloom breeds are generally those that have been left alone over the centuries to breed amongst themselves. They often maintain something of their original wildness, and they can survive extremes of heat and cold, scratch out a living on marginal real estate, and drop a lamb or two in the springtime with very little commotion. You won't enjoy huge legs of lamb or $100 fleeces from these animals, but you will certainly get both meat and wool from these breeds—albeit in less lucrative quantities than from their improved cousins.

The single best reason to choose an unimproved breed, in my opinion, is for their ease of lambing. Now don't be fooled: every breed is promoted by its boosters for its ease of lambing, for the obvious reason that promoting the opposite would be a deal killer. But giving every student in the class a straight A does not mean that all the students are equally bright, nor does labeling every breed as "easy lambing" mean that they all lamb about the same. Some shepherds feel that their breed lambs easily because the vet only has to be called once or twice a season. Others know that, with an unimproved breed, the vet never has to be called.

Well, hardly ever. The label *unimproved* by definition means that the breed has survived without much human selection: the lambs that survived were the ones who were born easily. If you are happy to trade away some potential revenue in order to enjoy a more peaceful lambing season, an unimproved breed may be for you.

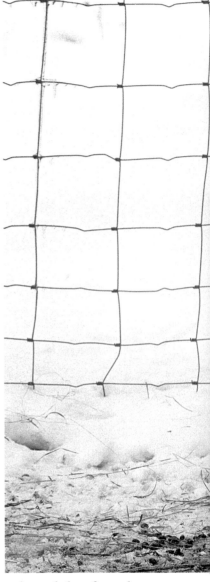

A second reason to choose an unimproved breed is to help safeguard some of the rarer sheep genetics that are in danger of being lost, thanks to the consolidation of industrial agriculture around a few preferred breeds. This isn't just hard work, it's also fun. These breeds have breeder associations

 Above: A Scottish Blackface ram keeps warm under his heavy coat of wool near a barn owned by John Lenihan in Strafford, Vermont. Lenihan usually has his small flock sheared in May.

and an animal registry along with a cadre of human enthusiasts who are working to prevent these breeds from becoming extinct. Plus, in this age of genetic manipulation, there's a certain faddishness to all things heirloom these days. You can buy or grow an amazing variety of heirloom tomatoes today—and the same applies to sheep.

Here's a list of the more common heirloom breeds:

Cotswold	Karakul	St. Croix
Finnsheep	Navajo-Churro	Tunis
Gulf Coast Native	Romanov	Welsh Mountain
Icelandic	Scottish Blackface	Wiltshire Horn
Jacob	Shetland	

The flock I bought from my friends turned out to be just such a breed—the Navajo-Churro. There are a dozen breeders of Navajo-Churro sheep in our part of Vermont, and it's been a nice added bonus to meet these people and be part of the effort to promulgate this rare and wonderful breed. We raise our sheep primarily for meat, and while our lambs are never as big as those from the commercial breeds, they sure are tasty. The wool from our sheep is also prized by handspinners, thanks to its length and range of natural colors, so I've been able to sell some wool too. Nina, in particular—one of the ewes that came to us in our original flock—has the most glorious milk chocolate–colored fleece. You won't find a color like that in any of the standard wool or meat breeds.

But being a shepherd of an heirloom breed is not without its drawbacks. First and foremost, any rams or ewes that you purchase for your flock also need to be registered purebreds. If not, your lambs won't be purebreds, either, and you won't be perpetuating the breed. The dozen breeders of Navajo-Churro in our area seem to be about the minimum number required to make it somewhat easy to buy and sell purebred animals and maintain the genetic diversity of our flocks.

Second, it's worth pausing at least once to inquire why a particular breed has become rare in the first place. Is it because the breed is not particularly hardy or thrifty or easy at lambing time? If so, you may face all the difficulties of the improved breeds without the financial payoff of great meat or great wool. The *purebred heirloom* moniker may be the selected trait, rather than ease of lambing, and unless you have the enthusiasm and skills to deal with the logistics of this, an heirloom breed may not be the best choice for the beginning shepherd. If there is a group of shepherds in your area that favors a particular heirloom breed, go for it. If not, I'd stick with one of the all-around purebreds I mentioned earlier.

DAIRY BREEDS

Most shepherds these days keep sheep for some combination of their wool, meat, or lawn-mowing skills. But a few brave souls keep sheep primarily for their milk. I don't call them brave souls to disparage sheep's milk in any way; it's just that, if you're going to go to the trouble of bringing an animal inside and getting it cleaned up for milking, you're going to get a heck of a lot more milk from a cow than from a sheep. As an article on sheep's cheese I recently read put it, sheep are shy producers.

Nevertheless, some of the world's great cheeses come exclusively (or usually) from sheep's milk, including feta, pecorino romano, Roquefort, ricotta, and more than a dozen others. Most sheep's milk goes into cheese making—both because you'd need a heck of a lot of sheep to launch a "Got milk?" campaign and because, at roughly twice the butterfat and solids of cow's milk, sheep's milk naturally lends itself to cheese making. All sheep breeds produce some amount of milk, but the most commonly milked sheep breeds are:

Assaf	Clun Forest	Lacaune
British Milksheep	East Friesian	

I'm not going to delve into the specifics of dairying in this book: like raising breeding stock and genetic selection, dairying is a specialized topic that deserves a book of its own. But there's nothing like a good, briny feta made from sheep's milk!

CROSSBREEDS

If you've already started talking with your neighbors or reading the classified ads, you've no doubt come across an amazing proliferation of crossbreeds for sale. These are listed something like, "Dorset X Romney." This is read as "Dorset crossed with Romney" or "Dorset-Romney cross." Many of these hybrids are simply the result of a shepherd buying a convenient ram one year that happened to be of a different breed than the ewes. Some crosses, however, are carefully considered hybrids that are intended to merge the best traits of two breeds and take advantage of *hybrid vigor*, the phenomenon (commonly observed in dogs and other species) in which mongrel offspring are both smarter and more vigorous than either of the original purebred parents.

If you're following the "keep it simple" approach of buying lambs in the spring for slaughter in the fall, a crossbreed is often a good way to go. These lambs, especially if their sire was from a top-tier meat breed, should grow rapidly to a nice, large size. If you're following the "glorified lawn mower" approach of keeping a few scenic sheep year-round, a crossbreed may also be your best bet, for they tend to be somewhat less expensive to purchase up front. Provided you aren't planning to use your animals for breeding, you can't go too wrong with a crossbreed: if the sheep look good, chances are they will be good.

But if you've "bought the farm" and you're planning to breed your sheep and raise your own lambs, you'd be well advised to stay away from the crossbreeds—at least at the outset. With a crossbreed, you don't necessarily know what you're in for come lambing time. In particular, one possibility

should be avoided at all costs: a large-breed ram having impregnated a small-breed ewe. You may as well schedule the vet several months in advance to come help deliver all the stuck lambs. Plus, unless you're an expert sheep geneticist, you'll have no idea what kind of animal you'll get if you breed one crossbreed with another. There are plenty of variables in play when starting a new flock of sheep; you'd do well to avoid the additional ones you'll get by choosing a crossbreed.

 Above: John O'Brien's flock of forty Romneys moves from one pasture to another at Landgoes Farm in Tunbridge, Vermont. His parents started the flock in the late 1950s with six sheep.

HOW MANY SHEEP CAN I HAVE AT MY PLACE?

The short answer: two sheep per acre of pasture. The long answer: I have no idea—and neither will you, at least at first.

There are too many variables that go into determining how many sheep you can graze in a given area. How good is the grass? Are there lots of legumes? Are the pastures being rotated? How much rain falls in your area in a regular year? How much has fallen this year? Is any falling right now? Did your sheep get into the pasture too early this spring and stunt the pasture's growth by nipping it in the bud? Or is this the first time there have been animals grazing on your land in a hundred years?

Lots of rain and rich soil means lots of grass and lots of sheep—maybe four or more animals per acre. Little rain on poor soil means just the opposite; even one sheep per acre could be too many.

In general, you want to have enough pasture available to feed your flock during the driest time of the year. If you overshoot on the numbers a little bit, you can always buy hay during the drought time—but then you are feeding your animals expensive hay instead of free pasture. Start small. If you are planning on raising your own lambs, it's easy to add more animals later. (In fact, it's nearly impossible not to!) It would be better to discover you never used your back pasture rather than scramble to feed a bunch of hungry mouths during a dry summer.

Whatever you do, don't look out your window, wave your hand up and down a few times, and decide you have five acres or so. Your acreage estimate will be more wrong than my two-sheep-per-acre estimate. Borrow a measuring wheel or a long tape measure and figure out exactly how much land you have. There are 43,560 square feet in an acre, which in layman's terms is a lot more area than you might think. Guessing that you have five acres when you have only three will get you into more trouble than you want to be in—and that's before the first sheep has set a hoof on your place.

FINAL NOTES BEFORE BUYING

There are a few key terms you'll want to know before you set out to buy your first sheep.

- **Registered purebred** means just what you'd think. These sheep are from a specific breed, and they have the certifying documents to prove they are listed in the breed registry. Dozens of breeds in the United States have a breed association, whose members maintain the official breed registry—a list of all the purebred animals of that breed in the U.S., along with their ancestors and bloodlines.

 Above: Romney ewe Lucinda looks for the rest of the flock at Landgoes Farm. While in college, John O'Brien took a year off to work on a 4,000-acre New Zealand farm, where the Romneys numbered 5,000.

- **Grade sheep** are those that may be purebreds but don't have the documents to prove it—often because one of the parents looks like a purebred but lacks the official paperwork.
- **Crossbreed sheep** are technically the offspring of two different pure breeds, as opposed to those that are a plain mélange of whatever happened to be available, for which a good term (like mutt) has yet to be coined in the ovine world.

If at all possible, bring an experienced hand with you when you're heading off to buy your flock—someone who knows what good sheep look like at a glance. Many potential faults are quite obvious: lameness, damaged hooves, missing teeth, face covered in wool, or malformed udder or testicles. Other flaws, such as overall conformation and how representative the animal is of its breed, will not be obvious to the uneducated eye.

Ewe lambs carry the genes that determine ease of lambing, mothering instincts, and, to a lesser extent, likelihood for multiple births. Choose ewes or ewe lambs that were born easily, had mothers that knew what to do, and were either twins or triplets.

Rams carry the genes for size, strength, and muscular development, so choose a ram or ram lambs that, most importantly, grew quickly and easily. If the ram was also a twin, so much the better. But it's less crucial for a ram to be a twin than it is for a ram to be large and strong.

Don't buy ewes that have already been bred and are "ready to go." That's a risky proposition. The obvious benefit of being pre-bred will be more than offset by the fact that you've never seen the ram and haven't the faintest idea of what's in store. Even worse, you won't know the date that it's likely to be in store. March? April? May sometime? Overall, I'd be extremely wary of any shepherd who went ahead and bred a flock without knowing that he or she would be around to see the process all the way through.

Don't buy your sheep at an auction—at least until you gain some experience. Sheep being sold at auction are invariably the ones the original shepherd didn't want and couldn't sell directly. It's all too easy to end up buying someone else's mistakes, and these mistakes are more apt to turn up (and harder to identify) at an auction than in the more deliberative setting of the seller's farm or ranch. Any "good deal" a novice buyer gets in the auction shed is—more than likely—an even better deal for the seller.

Finally, as I mentioned at the start of this chapter—and despite discussing the pros and cons of improved, hybrid, and unimproved or heirloom breeds—the best breed for getting started is still apt to be the one that your friend or neighbor is selling. Don't be too overwhelmed by

all the choices, make a decent selection from among the options in your area, and go for it! For reference, there's a complete list of all the purebred registries, associations, and some useful Web sites in the back of the book.

Above: A trio of Romneys graze at Landgoes Farm. John O'Brien grew up on the farm and has raised horses, cows, geese, pigs, goats, and chickens—but sheep have been on the farm since the late 1950s.

CHAPTER THREE
Where Your Sheep Will Live

Good sheep shelter, believe it or not, should be designed more for your benefit than for your flock's benefit. Sheep are a hardy lot: they've lived outdoors without our assistance for hundreds of thousands of years, they do pretty well in a wide variety of conditions, and their housing requirements are simple.

In the summer, sheep require shade—thanks in large part to our having bred them to produce so much wool. In the winter, they need a place to gather out of the wind and deep snow. That's about it. If your climate is warm and snow-free, summer shade will be more critial than winter shelter. If you can ski and sled on your pastures six months of the year, the opposite will be true. Keep the specifics of your own place and climate in mind as you read through this chapter.

Of course, your sheep will be happy to have more than the bare minimum. I've noticed our flock will usually avail themselves of a roof on rainy summer days, and they choose the barn on cold winter nights. If it's easy for you to provide these amenities, so much the better. But my overall point is that your sheep do not require living arrangements that are fancy or expensive. It's just as important that these living arrangements work well for you.

 Opposite: Some Katahdin sheep take refuge from the morning humidity at Wetmore farm.

SUMMER SHELTER

Summer is the simpler season. Your flock's main concern is finding shade, which you can provide most easily by making sure there are trees adjacent to their pasture area. Notice that I said *adjacent to*. Sheep are notorious rubbers; they won't attack trees with the devious intent of their equine cousins, but they will rub against tree trunks if given the chance and can easily girdle and kill trees—especially young ones with sap under the bark in the springtime. If you have trees within your proposed pasture areas, put a ring of posts and fencing around the trunks to protect them from damage.

From the shepherd's perspective, the shade provided by trees (in addition to being cheap and already installed) has the added advantage of moving about during the day as the sun tracks across the sky. This means that your sheep will move about too, which minimizes the extent to which any one area of pasture becomes excessively muddy or covered with manure.

But there is a limit to how far you want to go in taking advantage of natural shade. Old-school shepherds used to release their sheep into wooded areas adjacent to their pastures. This nicely solved the shade problem, but it did nothing for the woodlands and the wildlife. Unless you are planning to convert a wooded area into a new pasture (a task for which sheep are well suited), keep your sheep out of the woods. The money you think you are saving on cheap shade is money you are actually losing many times over by damaging your woodlot, to say nothing of the damage to the habitat of ground-nesting birds and critters caused by ovine hooves and mouths.

If natural shade isn't available on your farm, or if you don't want to defoliate your forest, then you will need to provide some sort of roof to protect your sheep from the sun. This could be anything from a barn or

shelter that houses your sheep in winter to a simple shade canopy set up just for this purpose in the summer. Before you choose, think what would best meet your needs.

For the first few years we had sheep, I set up the fencing so the flock could always make it back into the shade of the barn during the day—regardless of where they happened to be grazing. I did this without

 Above: During a hot and humid summer morning, a Suffolk lamb finds relief in the shade of a lean-to at Harlow Brook Farm. This pasture is far from the barn, so the improvised lean-to serves as a shade shelter.

 Above: Sobe, a Navajo-Churro ewe originally from New Mexico, rests in the spring sun at The Land & Lamb Co. in Tunbridge, Vermont. Sheep can easily kill trees by rubbing and eating their bark. In this case, the damage was desirable: the owner is using the sheep to reclaim this former pasture.

really thinking about it. The shade was in the barn, and the sheep needed to get to the shade. The fact that I had to string several hundred yards of fencing to link the fields with the barn didn't enter into my thinking. Neither did the barn full of stinky manure on a summer day when the temperature reached 90°F.

Winter affords ample time for reflection and speculation, and one winter day while I was staring out across the snow-covered pasture, it dawned on me: I'd be ahead of the game if I brought the shade to the sheep instead of bringing the sheep to the shade. So I bought a portable shade canopy (the kind people use for carports and temporary garages) and more than made that money

back the following summer in time I didn't spend moving portable fences around and mucking out the barn. If you don't have a local source for buying a portable canopy, search the Internet for a "portable shade canopy." (See the appendix for a complete list of tools and equipment.)

My point is not that you should rush out and buy yourself a portable shade canopy. (They are kind of ugly—and I hope one day to replace mine with a more quaint-looking wooden structure.) Rather, you should take time to think about the specifics of your situation. If your farm comes with a barn already on it, is that barn in the right place? Is the place you plan to house the sheep in winter the most convenient place for them to be in the summer? Would separate summer and winter quarters be far easier and less expensive than trying to make one shelter work year-round?

In my case, having separate summer and winter quarters works well for two reasons: shade and manure. My flock's winter quarters are an old dairy barn that came with our place. It's a lovely old farm building and very pleasing to the eye, but it's a devil to shovel manure out of. (I'm surmising that the old-time dairy farmer had several sets of younger hands available to help with this regular task.) But now that my flock spends six months of the year outside in their summer quarters, I'm pleased to report that I no longer shovel manure out of the barn as often as I used to.

As I alluded to earlier, your summer shelter needs to be set up so it's easy for your sheep to access their summer pastures. Good grazing practices require a fair bit of moving sheep from one pasture to another (see more in chapter 4). If it is easy for you to rotate sheep between paddocks and pastures, you're likely to do it often and to great advantage. If not, you won't. So take some time to think through the permutations of

Above: Navajo-Churro sheep gather under a portable shade canopy at Sunrise Farm in Hartford, Vermont. Typically used as carports, these shade canopies can also be a quick and inexpensive way to bring summer shade to distant pastures.

pasture, manure, shade, and water before you come to any final conclusions about summer shelter. Or you may be like me and use a less-than-optimal situation for a few years—until inspiration strikes and reveals a better plan.

WINTER SHELTER

Winter shelter is somewhat more complicated than summer shelter. First and foremost, sheep need protection from the wind. Wool sweaters are famously warm, even when wet; but when was the last time you wore a wool sweater on a windy day without some sort of outer wind-proof shell? Sheep don't wear windbreakers, and although they can cook away contentedly at twenty below zero, their heat can be sucked away by gusts of wind. You need to provide them with some sort of refuge.

Visitors to our barn in winter often view me as a villain for leaving the doors and windows open, even on the coldest nights. The sheep often have frost on their outer coats, or even snow or ice if they've been outside much. But I just make a point of having my horrified visitors press their fingers deep into the wool to feel the heat trapped next to the animal's skin. What better advertisement for wool is there?

Your goal is to provide wind shelter for your sheep without confining them to quarters so tight that no air moves around. Sheep need fresh air for optimum health; and since few shepherds clean the barn as often in the winter as might be ideal, make sure that there is plenty of airflow through your barn or shelter. As long as it's not windy, it's fine.

The second winter-shelter concern for sheep is deep snow: you need to make sure they don't get trapped in it. Sheep are squat animals on stubby legs (think of the moose, for example, if you want an idea of a long-legged ungulate better adapted to living in snow). If the snow becomes much deeper than a sheep's belly, the animal is likely to founder and flail. This may not necessarily cause them to get stuck, but it's needlessly stressful and unhelpful for the animal. In the worst case, if they do become stuck they can easily freeze to death.

Depending on how cold and snowy your winters are, effective winter shelter may be as simple as the windbreak provided by the side of a building. If snow tends to pile up where you live, a shed roof off the side of a building will, at a minimum, be required. If you decide to construct a freestanding shed or pole barn, it ought to have one, two, or three sides closed in—depending on how windy your site is and whether or not the wind reliably blows from a constant direction. If you already have an existing barn on your farm, as we did, then you're all set. Just make sure there's enough airflow through the barn by leaving doors and windows open as needed.

In general, plan on providing a minimum of ten square feet of floor space per animal in their winter quarters, whether you choose a windbreak, a shed, or a barn. Sheep can certainly be physically squeezed into a smaller space, but I find that our sheep will rarely lie down cheek to jowl if they aren't forced to. Fifteen square feet per animal is better. Sheep like to be able to move around their shelter without having to step on one another or be forced to confront a higher-ranking member of the flock who might happen to be sleeping in front of the water dish.

From your perspective, the trickiest part of winter shelter is manure, which can pile up almost as fast as the snow. A full-grown ewe can produce six to eight pounds of pellets per day, and that's not counting the bedding you'll be adding for their health and comfort. Here's where a simple windbreak or three-sided shelter can earn its keep; it'll be easy for you to get in there with a tractor, wheelbarrow, a pickup truck, or whatever system you've devised for removing the winter manure to a more acceptable location.

Winter Manure Management

There are two schools of thought on how best to manage manure in winter: the thin-bed school and the thick-bed school. Thin-bed schoolers throw

inspired house

www.inspiredhouse.com

☐ **1 year** (6 issues) only **$24.95**
You'll save 41%*

☐ **2 years** (12 issues) **$41.95**
You'll save 50%*

☐ **3 years** (18 issues) **$57.95**
You'll save 54%*

Total amount due:

$ _____

Payable in U.S. funds. Above prices for U.S. and
Canadian residents (GST included). Outside the
U.S./Canada: $31/yr; $54/2 yrs.; $76/3 yrs.
*Savings off U.S. newsstand price.

☐ Payment enclosed.

☐ MasterCard/Visa   ☐ AmEx   ☐ Discover

Charge-card # _____

☐ Please bill me.

Subscribe & Save:

Name _____

Address _____ Apt. # _____

City _____ State _____ Zip _____

Email _____

Give a Gift & Save: (please include your name and address above)

Send to _____

Address _____ Apt. # _____

City _____ State _____ Zip _____

Sign Gift Card From: _____

_____ Exp. date _____ Initials _____

Offer ends 2/28/06

Create a home that works for you!

Inspired
house

Subscribe now!

down a minimum of bedding for their sheep **Above:** Shetland lambs and completely sweep the shelter out every few days. Thick-bed schoolers just throw new bedding on top of old and deal with the whole pile at once, in the spring. Naturally, there are advantages and disadvantages to both approaches.

The advantage of the thin-bed approach is that you never have to deal with a stinky pile of manure, since oxygen can get into the bedding. Sheep manure does not smell

Above: Shetland lambs graze near the "ovine condos" at Maple Ridge Sheep Farm. Used to house the farm's flock of 200 sheep in the winter, these buildings are moved around with a tractor in the summer to clean out the manure.

Above: Three Scottish Blackface sheep eat grain in a three-sided barn at the Lenihans' farm, which was originally built by their son as a high school project for their single cow, who died at age seventeen of old age.

particularly pungent on its own; it's only when sheep manure has been piled up in oxygen-deprived conditions that it starts to smell strongly of ammonia.

The disadvantage of the thin-bed approach is that you have to clean the shelter out all the time. Even if each sweep-out isn't particularly difficult, it's still time you need to spend on a regular basis. The key here is how easy it is to sweep out the old bedding. If it's as simple as sweeping a concrete floor out the side of an open shed, that's one thing. If it involves a wheelbarrow or tractor or a long haul, that's another.

The thick-bed schoolers have very little regular maintenance to attend to. They simply throw down a little fresh bedding on top of the old stuff when it becomes dirty or sodden, maybe once every week or so. Come springtime, however, the piper must be paid, and a six- to eight-inch-thick mat of manure and sodden bedding needs to be dealt with before rising temperatures and the accompanying rising odors make the whole area unbearable for sheep and shepherd alike. If it's difficult for you to sweep your shelter out on a regular basis but easy to get a truck or tractor into position once the snow has melted, the thick-bed approach may be for you. That's how it is at our farm. I make a point of waiting for the first weekend afternoon game of the spring baseball season to, as it were, dive on in.

Bedding

Whichever school of manure management you subscribe to—thin bed or thick bed—you'll need to provide some bedding for your sheep so they aren't lying directly on the floor or ground in the winter, which will be both unduly cold and dirty for them. If your shelter has a dirt floor so that the urine can soak into the ground all winter, then spreading hay around will do the trick nicely. Mulch hay is generally inexpensive and widely available. Plan on spending a dollar or two per bale, and buying one to two bales per sheep for the winter.

If your ultimate goal with your sheep is to sell the wool, however, you'll find that hay tends to get stuck in the wool and makes cleaning a fleece quite arduous. Use straw instead: the long stalks tend not to get stuck in wool as easily and can be removed later as needed. Despite the extra cost (straw can run from four to eight dollars per bale), you'll make up that money and more in time not spent extracting tiny seed heads from your prized fleeces.

If your shelter has a wood or concrete floor, sawdust is the bedding of choice because it absorbs urine so nicely. A little hay on top helps keep the sawdust in place; straw would be the ultimate choice here, too, for keeping wool clean. Wood shavings also work well and can generally be purchased from feed stores in bags. If you have a sawmill or woodshop nearby, you can often purchase sawdust or shavings by the truckload for a very reasonable price, for these businesses are often looking to get rid of the stuff. A truckload will last you several years, assuming you have a place to store the sawdust or shavings before using them.

Finally, if you adhere to the thick-bed school of manure management, use some lime every now and again to keep odors to a minimum. Your shelter will always smell like sheep, but it shouldn't smell like ammonia. I like to spread a thin dusting of lime on top of the old bedding before adding a new layer, or spread it directly on the floor. The lime won't hurt the sheep: it will reduce the amount of ammonia they end up breathing in, and it will also sweeten the manure should you compost it in the summer. One 50 pound bag of lime will be plenty for a dozen sheep for one winter.

Recycling Winter Manure

The value of manure is in the eye of the beholder—so I urge you to see a mountain of gold where others see a pile of crap. Manure mixed with bedding is ideal material for making compost. Rather than pushing your manure over a bank and washing your hands of the stuff, consider composting it. Not only will you have the best fertilizer for your lawn, gardens, or pastures that money can buy, but also you will capture the natural fertility of the manure and prevent it from leaching out and potentially polluting nearby streams or ponds.

All you have to do to make compost is make a pile out of your manure/bedding mix and turn it over every month or so during the summer to allow it to aerate. If you have a tractor on hand, this will only take a few minutes, as will turning it by shovel if you only have three sheep or so. If you have a larger flock and no tractor, figure out how to borrow or rent one for the job. Or quit your day job and become a shoveler.

When autumn comes, you'll notice when you turn the pile that it looks a lot like dirt and no longer has that pungent ammonia smell of fresh manure. At that point, it's ready to go. I like to spread all of my compost in the fall on our vegetable and flower beds before the ground freezes, so it can start working itself into the soil in time for spring.

If you're looking for ways to add to your shepherding bottom line, take a trip to your local nursery or garden store and see how much a small bag of composted manure will set you back. Three sheep minding their own business through the winter can easily crank out a hundred dollars or more of finished compost.

 Above: Although they're outside during the day in the winter, sheep at Fat Rooster Farm are kept inside the barn's winter paddock during lambing and while the lambs are young.

CHAPTER FOUR

Feeding Your Sheep

I used to think that feeding sheep would be among the easiest of the shepherding tasks: you buy some hay, maybe some grain, and away you go. In a way, that's true. It is easy. But feeding sheep is also the most crucial of the shepherd's tasks. Get it right, and your animals will be happy and healthy. Get it wrong, and your sheep will turn up with an amazing assortment of seemingly unrelated maladies: from bloating in summer, to freezing in the winter, to problems with lambing, hooves, and lameness.

Complicating matters is the fact that feeding your sheep correctly is, at times, a counter-intuitive task. Sheep are ruminants—stalwart members of the multiple-stomached, vegetarian, cud-chewing clan—whose digestive tracts require stability and constancy for optimal performance. We humans are opportunistic omnivores who delight in variety and view the prospect of eating the same meal day after day with loathing and despair. This sets the stage for the classic mistake of the beginning shepherd: projecting human food desires onto those of our ovine companions.

The good news is that, while feeding your sheep may be a matter of life and death, your sheep will do everything possible to help you get it right. Your sheep, by and large, know what is good for them and will offer constant advice and suggestions. Your job is simply to pay attention, learn to understand sheep-speak, and make adjustments as necessary.

Opposite: Marian White's Navajo-Churro ewes graze in a neighbor's pasture in the summer. It's mutually beneficial; White's sheep eat fresh grass and her neighbor's land remains open, free of brush.

 Above: A forty-animal Romney flock grazes on fifteen acres of pasture at Landgoes Farm.

Here's the big picture: sheep eat grass. That means pasture in the summer and hay in the winter. (Hay, of course, is nothing but pasture that was harvested in advance to see the flock through the winter months when the pastures are covered in snow.) Sheep love grass and will eat it every day of the year if given the chance. Beyond grass, sheep need water and minerals. These are the big three: grass, water, and minerals. Notice that I haven't said anything yet about grain, which I'll cover later in the chapter.

But here's something of a curveball: although sheep eat grass, they don't digest it. What sheep do, instead, is create favorable conditions in their digestive tracts for a whole host of microbes and organisms that break the roughage down into simpler forms that the sheep's digestive systems can then absorb and use. (Sheep aren't the only animals to have figured this out; all the cud-chewing ungulates do the same.) Sheep have a four-part stomach in which the first three parts are devoted to the care and feeding of the microbe economy and only the fourth is roughly akin to the human stomach.

The first chamber of the ovine stomach system is called the *rumen*, from which the term *ruminant* was derived as a name for the earth's cud chewers. Chewing cud, incidentally, is a sophisticated way of grabbing a quick meal on the run. With a wary eye out for trouble, sheep stuff their faces with grass and store it in their rumens; they regurgitate it later, when the coast is clear, so it can be chewed and enjoyed at leisure. This strikes me as far more civilized than the burping-through-the drive-through routine that so many of us humans now endure, with no time available for rumination.

The take-home message for you, the shepherd, is you need to pay attention to the care and feeding of your sheep's digestive microbes, not just to the sheep themselves. "Make no sudden moves" is the golden rule of feeding sheep. It takes time for the microbial populations inside an animal's gut to react to changes in feed, which means that anytime you change the amount or type of food your sheep are eating, you want to do so over the course of several days and not all at once. Look for more on this later in the chapter, once we've taken a closer look at the big three: grass, water, and minerals.

PASTURE

Pasture is free grass, at least if you are going to be paying property taxes on your fields anyway. Pasture is also the very best food for your sheep to eat, for it's loaded with vitamins and minerals. Put these two together, and you should aim to have your sheep on pasture as much of the year as possible.

The art and science of pasture management fills many volumes on the interested shepherds bookshelf. Indeed, an increasing number of shepherds refer to themselves as grass farmers, and not sheep farmers, to acknowledge the key role that grass plays in a productive livestock operation. At its best, good pasture management turns something free—sunlight and rain—into something of great value, sheep. At its worst (and you'll come to know it when you see it), pasture management can turn naturally fertile soil into land that has been stripped of its wealth and nutrients and is unfit for ovine occupation.

The worst-case scenario is this: take a large number of sheep, fence them into a small pasture, and sit back and relax. No further effort will be required on your part to turn your land into a disaster area. The second-worst-case scenario is almost as easy: fence a small number of sheep into a big pasture and, once again, sit back and relax. After a few years, your sheep will be sick and starving and your land will be wrecked.

Sheep, like many humans, prefer to eat dessert first. Turn them out in a pasture that has some nice, tasty alfalfa interspersed with some decent grass and an occasional thorny thistle, and they'll eat the alfalfa. Then they'll work on the grass. But they'll never eat the thistle. Allow this to go on long enough, and you'll have a pasture with no alfalfa, some sparse grass, and lots of thistle. Your sheep can start to starve, even in a large pasture, because they've "high-graded" the pasture by taking the best and leaving the rest.

Crowd a large number of sheep into a small pasture, and the effect will be even worse. They still won't eat the thistle, but they'll eat everything else down to its roots and kill it in the process. You'll have a nice dust bowl full of thistle, with your natural topsoil blowing away in the wind or washing away in the rain.

In the wild, of course, ungulates avoid wreaking havoc like this by being able to move on to greener pastures every now and again; the herd descends on a lush valley, eats it down to the ground, and then moves on, allowing the forage to regrow. The key to successful pasture management, therefore, is to mimic this natural process through a technique commonly known as *rotational grazing*.

ROTATIONAL GRAZING

As the name suggests, rotational grazing means rotating the grazing between different pastures. Your goal is to mimic the sudden arrival and departure of the herd. When the herd is there, they eat almost everything—including stuff they don't necessarily like too much, because they are crowded and food is scarce. But when they're gone, the pasture has a chance to recover and grow back without being constantly nibbled. Done properly, rotational grazing will improve the quality of the pasture, the quantity of the forage, and the health and happiness of your sheep. You'll have more sheep, bigger sheep, happier sheep.

The standard approach to rotational grazing is to divide your pasture space into a number of smaller pastures using either permanent or portable fencing (more on how to do this in the next chapter). On some sort of regular schedule, you move your flock from one pasture to the next over the course of the grazing season, allowing each pasture to grow back between visits.

If your nascent shepherding I.Q. is particularly high, the combination of the terms *regular schedule* and *grow back* in the previous sentence will have caused dark clouds to gather in your mind. Indeed, as anyone who has ever wielded a lawn mower intuitively knows, grass does not grow back on a regular schedule. It grows a lot when the weather is wet and cool, and it grows not at all when the weather is scorching and dry. To address this problem, the current lingo in the shepherding world is about *intensively managed grazing* instead of rotational grazing.

Intensively Managed Grazing

Under intensively managed grazing, the shepherd's chief goal is to grow grass—not feed sheep. This may seem like a fine distinction. But just like the idea of focusing on feeding the sheep's microbes instead of the sheep themselves, growing grass instead of feeding sheep is a very useful concept for helping the beginning shepherd get it right.

The theory is this: pasture grass grows very little in the first few days after it's been grazed, because it's gathering energy from its roots to begin regrowth. Once new growth begins, grass grows very rapidly for several weeks until it reaches maturity; once maturity is reached, grass grows more slowly because it puts energy into reproduction and seed instead of into new leaves and height. If the shepherd can arrange to have the sheep on a pasture only during the steep, middle part of the growth curve, the amount (and quality) of the pasture can be maximized. In other words, put the sheep in when the grass is tall and about to go to seed and pull them out before any regrowth begins.

If you guessed that keeping track of your various pastures could quickly become a full- time job, you're right. But if you're not inclined to become a serious student of intensively managed grazing—and I, so far, have not—there are two quick and dirty rules to help you decide when it's time to move your sheep from one pasture to the next: the $^2/_{10}$ rule, and the five-day rule. Both are very straightforward.

The $^2/_{10}$ rule states simply that sheep should start grazing a pasture before the grasses reach ten inches in height and should be removed from

the pasture before they've eaten the grasses down to two inches in height. More prosaically, the $^2/_{10}$ rule is also the boot-top rule: put the sheep in when the grass is up to the top of your boots (high-topped rubber Wellingtons, that is) and take them out when it is grazed down to just over the toe of your boot.

 Above: Sombrero, a Navajo-Churro ewe, munches on pasture. Done properly, rotational grazing improves the quality and quantity of the forage as well as the health and happiness of the flock.

Feeding Your Sheep **49**

The five-day rule states that sheep should not spend more than five days doing this on any one pasture. If the pasture is taking more than five days to be eaten down, the pasture space is too big. If it's taking less than five days, that's perfectly fine. It just means that you'll be moving your sheep around more often than you absolutely have to. I've visited a dairy farm where they move the fencing every twelve hours so that, each time the cows come back out of the milking parlor, they always go to fresh grass. The farmers create very small pastures using electric fencing, and the herd eats everything down to two inches before going in for the next milking.

I find that the number five is rather awkward for a part-time shepherd like myself, living in the seven-day week we humans have created. Rather than move my sheep on Wednesday this week, Monday next week (and then forgetting to move them the following Saturday when I'm away for the weekend), I aim to move them twice per week on a fixed schedule. Monday and Thursday work well for me, meaning that the sheep have three days and then four days between pastures. In the heart of the summer when grass growth is slowing down, I violate the five-day rule (and lose some efficiency in grass regrowth) by moving the flock only once per week. It's a heck of a lot easier to remember "Monday is move-the-sheep day" than trying to recall when I last moved them and wondering whether today is the day.

In order to pull off an intensively managed grazing system like this, portable electric fencing is almost essential. As you can imagine, the amount of area needed to feed your flock for five days will be much smaller during the flush of spring than during the drought of summer. Portable fencing allows you to constantly adjust your pasture size each time you move your sheep.

A system like this also requires you to have some sort of mower to knock down all the excess grass in late spring that your sheep won't be able to keep up with. If you don't cut it, the grass will go to seed, turn brown, and be far less attractive to your flock come August, when they'll need to graze on it as regrowth slows in other areas. If you have a tractor and mower, so much the better. If not, call a neighbor who does and see if you can persuade him or her to lend you a hand in late spring by cutting any pasture that your sheep didn't get to.

If this sounds like a lot of work, it can be. Intensively managed or rotational grazing takes a lot more effort than just turning your sheep out into a big pasture for the summer. You may not want to do all this work; you may just want to have a few sheep on your land to keep the grass down and improve the pastoral view from your porch. That's fine. You should just realize two things: first, you'll need to use a tractor every year to mow the pasture and beat down all the tough stuff the sheep haven't eaten; second, as the pasture deteriorates over time, you'll need to either make a bigger pasture, run fewer sheep, or add lime and compost every now and then to help the grasses hold on.

ADDING LIME

Adding lime every now and then isn't a bad idea, regardless of your approach to pasture management. Lime is simply ground up limestone— either calcium carbonate or magnesium carbonate. Rainfall in temperate climates tends to be naturally acidic. Throw in the additional acidity that we humans put into the air by burning so much fossil fuel, and the result is that our annual rains tend to strip calcium and other essential nutrients from the soil—especially the top few inches of soil where pasture grasses grow. As these minerals are leached away and the soil becomes more acidic, legumes like alfalfa and clover (that your sheep love) will die out and be replaced by much tougher grasses and weeds.

The solution to this problem is to spread lime on your field—either by hand if your pasture is small, or by hiring a company to come and do it with a truck. The first step is to do a soil test to determine the acidity of your pasture right now. This typically involves mailing a small sample off to a laboratory for analysis; your agricultural extension office is a good place to start for finding out how and where to do this. Once the results come back, you'll know how much lime is required to restore optimal fertility to your pasture.

The soil test results may also tell you about other nutrients and minerals you could spread on your pasture to improve the quality of the forage.

Whether or not you take these additional steps is up to you. Provided you are giving your sheep access to supplemental minerals with their feed, they won't need to get these minerals from the pasture. Adding these amendments to your soil, however, will certainly increase the quantity and quality of the forage you are growing and may lead to bigger sheep, faster growth, or your ability to put more sheep on the same sized pasture. Decide for yourself whether or not it's worth it—but don't worry about it in the first year or two while you are getting started.

POISONOUS PLANTS

While you're out scouting your pastures and doing soil tests, keep an eye out for poisonous plants that may make your sheep ill. A field guide can help you to identify these. The list of such plants isn't long, and the occasional mouthful of most of these plants won't do any serious harm. But you do want to make sure that your sheep aren't out grazing in a meadow full of any one of these plants. (If you discover this after the fact, and your sheep are starting to behave oddly, call the vet right away.) The most common culprits are:

Rose family trees (CHERRY, SERVICEBERRY)	Beets and chard	Milkweed
	Lupine seeds	Rhubarb
Nightshade family, INCLUDING TOMATOES, POTATOES, AND PEPPERS	Skunk cabbage	Pigweed
	St. Johnswort	
Buckwheat	Goldenrod	

If you discover that a part of your pasture has been commandeered by one of these villains, either mow the pasture far enough in advance so the offending foliage will have withered and desiccated before the flock moves in, or simply pull the plants out by hand if the scoundrels are few in number. A farmer I know hereabouts used to pay his nieces and nephews a penny a plant for each milkweed stem they pulled out. I have yet to try this scheme on my nephews, but I suspect the price has gone up in recent years.

HAY

Hay is the stuff you feed your sheep in the off-season when they can't eat pasture. Depending on where you live, this off-season can be anywhere from a few short months to half a year.

You've probably made it this far in life believing that one bale of hay was the same

 Above: From left, a bale of straw (yellow), second-cut hay (green), and mulch hay (brown) show differences in texture and color at Sunrise Farm. The straw and mulch hay are used for bedding for Navajo-Churro sheep and the second-cut hay is used for feed.

 Above: John Lenihan spreads a partial bale of hay under the watchful eye of Tiger, a Scottish Blackface ram.

as the next, but your newly opened shepherd's eyes are about to discover a universe of variety in this thing called hay. Understanding this variety is essential for getting the right food for your sheep at the right time.

There's first-cut hay, second-cut hay, and third-cut hay. This jargon simply refers to how many times a hayfield is being cut in a given year, and which cutting the hay in question came from. In general, second-cut hay is the best for feeding sheep.

First-cut hay can be harvested anytime from late spring, in which case it will be chock-full of tender green blades of grass, to anytime before the snow flies, in which case it will be tough—all brown stems and seed heads. Second-cut hay is likely to be more uniform than first-cut hay because it's mostly tender regrowth. Third-cut hay can also be very uniform—but it can be very poor quality stuff if it's from a field being strip-mined of nutrients and not properly fertilized.

Although second-cut is usually best for sheep—who love tender green leaves and eschew tough brown stems—the thing to watch for is the color of the bale. Green is good, brown is bad. A greener-colored hay has more protein than a browner-colored hay—and in general, you're looking for greener rather than browner hay. Sure, the sheep experts at your local extension office have a lot more to say about hay quality than its color. But if you are getting your feet in the door as a beginning shepherd, the green/brown distinction won't let you down. There'll be plenty of time ahead to become a forage expert if you so desire.

Bad second-cut hay can be worse than good first-cut or third-cut hay—especially if it wasn't dried, baled, and brought under cover quickly. Likewise, first-cut hay that was harvested when the grass was young and lush can be fabulous stuff—the best there is—and much better than mishandled second-cut. Keep the green/brown distinction in mind, and go for the green.

Besides green versus brown, when you look closely at the individual grasses in a bale of hay, you want to see some leaves in there and not just stems and seeds. Green leaves are the good stuff your sheep will love. In general, good quality hay will feel soft to the touch, even when you press your hand against the rough side of the bale. If it's the sort of thing that seems suitable for a roll in the hay, you've got your stuff. If all you can think about is lacerations and cuts, look elsewhere.

How Much Hay to Buy

For planning purposes, you should buy four pounds of hay per animal per day to comfortably see your flock through the winter. To figure out what you'll need for your entire flock for the winter, multiply the number of animals in your flock by four to figure out how many pounds you'll need per day; then multiply that figure by the number of days in your winter. That equation will tell you roughly how many pounds of hay you'll need. Make sure you use the number of days in your longest conceivable winter—there's nothing fun about running out of hay in early spring when the roads are muddy, the barnyard is a mess, and nobody has any hay left to sell. You can always use leftover hay for bedding or mulch the following year.

The classic square bale of hay is said to weigh forty pounds, though that weight can be as little as thirty pounds from an old or maladjusted baler. Divide your total hay needs by thirty or forty pounds to determine a range of how many square bales you'll need. Once you see and heft one of the bales you are actually going to buy, you'll know the final number that you need. Then round up. If this is your first winter in the shepherding biz, you'd much rather be long on hay rather than short.

Many farmers today are converting to the larger round bales of hay, which can weigh several hundred pounds. These don't seem particularly convenient to me unless your flock is big enough to be going through a full bale every couple of days or so. If you do decide (or need to, because that's what every farmer in your area is doing) to go this large-bale route, remember that the bales are too large to be maneuvered by hand. Either use a tractor or truck in the fall to store the bales exactly where you'll need them in the winter; or have a tractor available through the winter for moving them around.

Following up on that thought, you'll want to store your hay as close to the animals' mouths as possible. You'll be much happier if you go to the trouble of putting your hay in the right spot in the fall—before snow and cold set in—as opposed to having to move hay long distances throughout the winter. Keep in mind that your definition of "long distances" will become quite short as January drags on into February.

Other than that, make sure your hay stays dry in storage. If it gets wet, it will rot and lose its nutritive value to the sheep. If it gets wet, it may also begin to compost and heat up, eventually even spontaneously combusting (far more barns have burned down from hay combustion than from so-called lightning strikes). If you're storing your hay on the ground or on the ground

floor of a barn, throw some scrap wood or pallets down under the hay to allow air to circulate and prevent spoilage. Finally, store your hay in a reasonably dark place. Light, especially direct sunlight, will also cause your hay to age and decompose prematurely.

If you are already a seasoned hay-maker with all the land, tools, and expertise required for making your own hay, go for it. Otherwise, don't make your own hay! There will be plenty of time later to invest your thousands and learn how difficult it can be to make hay. In the meantime, keep your

 Above: Paris, a purebred Southdown ram, looks up from eating hay at Fat Rooster Farm. To control their weight, sheep can either eat smaller amounts of rich hay or larger quantities of lower grade hay.

focus on the sheep and enjoy the chance to dicker with your neighborhood farmers about weather, price, and quality. You're going to get to know these people anyway—and it's either going to be standing around their hay wagon haggling over price, or underneath the belly of your busted baler trying to fix it. You'll make a better impression if it's the former.

One final note when buying hay: is it dry? If the hay was baled wet, it will rot and can possibly make your sheep sick and expose you to the aforementioned risk of a barn fire. The grass in a good, dry bale of hay should be crinkly, not soggy. And a "forty-pound bale" shouldn't be too heavy to lift because of an extra few dozen pounds of water. If this is the case, go elsewhere for your hay.

How to Feed Hay

The best way to feed hay to your sheep is to throw it down on snow-covered ground and let them bend down to eat it, just as if they were eating pasture. This gets your animals out of the barn and exercising; it also gets them pooping outside instead of inside. Having your sheep eat off of the snow also keeps their fleeces cleaner, since the hay is always below them. This is a major consideration if you have plans for working with or selling their wool.

Make sure you move your feeding spot around as the winter progresses, possibly packing down snow with snowshoes or plowing out a section of barnyard as the snow deepens. If you always throw the hay down in the same general area, you'll discover come springtime that a thick mat of leftover hay stems is killing the pasture underneath it. Plus, your sheep will have been eating hay atop poop-riddled snow.

If it's very windy or if there's no snow on the ground, however, you'll need some sort of feeder inside the barn or shelter. As a general rule, you'll want to provide between sixteen and twenty linear inches of feeder space per animal when designing your feeder. My wooly sheep need all twenty inches in late winter, when their volume is effectively doubled by their long wool; but they need only sixteen inches or less starting the moment the shearer has left. Your sheep will want to

Opposite: Ivan the Scottish Blackface ram eats hay outside the Lenihan's barn. The Lenihans feed hay twice a day in the winter months.

eat together as a group; having too little feeder space means that your smallest and weakest sheep will be forced out, to their great distress. These are generally the animals you are trying to get the most food to, so too little feeder space is a problem to avoid. Too much feeder space is not a problem at all, unless you're building the thing out of top-dollar, imported mahogany or something.

I built our hay feeder against one of the inside walls of the shelter pen so I can feed the flock without having to step into their pen. (This is very convenient if you're about to head off into town in street shoes and don't want to walk on soiled bedding.) Using scrap wood, I made a level shelf about eight inches deep that's twenty inches off the ground. The hay scraps fall onto this shelf, which has a one-inch-high lip to minimize spillage. I've left a gap in the lip every four feet or so. Before each feeding, I sweep out the chaff and any debris that the sheep don't eat to keep the feeder clean and tidy.

Above the shelf, I made a slatted rack that holds the flakes of hay and allows the sheep to pull hay out as they want it. I originally made this out of scrap wood, with the slats about ten inches apart. But I've since upgraded to a steel mesh panel that requires the sheep to pull harder to get the hay (see the list of tools and equipment in the back of the book for more information about the steel panel and possible feeder designs). I found that the wooden slats allowed the hay to fall through too easily, and the sheep would waste a fair bit either by biting off more than they could chew or by dropping it on each other's heads and necks while chewing. Whether you use wood or steel, make this rack vertical, or nearly so; you want the sheep to pull the hay out toward them, not down on top of them where it will lodge in their fleeces.

Alternatively, you can make or buy a whole-bale feeder that allows the sheep to eat from whole bales over the course of several days. These feeders can be placed either inside or, if they have covers of some sort, outside the shelter. Whole-bale feeders have the advantage of requiring a refill only every now and again, especially if you have no more than five or six sheep per feeder. They also keep the fleeces clean since the sheep are reaching down to get the hay, just like they do when they graze in the summer.

How Much Hay to Feed

Three to three-and-a-half pounds per sheep per day is the standard ration for healthy, adult sheep in the middle of the winter. But your sheep will gladly overeat if given the opportunity, and three pounds may not be the right number all the time. (You will notice I recommend buying four pounds of hay. This is because during breeding and lambing, you'll be feeding more. Between this and the likelihood of some waste and spoilage, you should buy four just to be safe.) The first winter with my flock, when I knew very little about hay quality, I bought a truckload of second-cut hay, sight unseen, and fed my ewes four pounds of it each day. I didn't know they could overeat; but when the shearer came in the spring, and we could see them without their wool, he told me they were all in perfect condition. Hey, this is easy!

The second winter, knowing more about hay, I bought a truckload of luscious second-cut hay from my neighbor after examining a few of the bales on the wagon. It was quality stuff. I still didn't know about sheep gaining too much weight, however, so I fed them the four pounds per day. When the shearer arrived in the spring, whoa! The fat that draped on the hips of the ewes was obvious even to the untrained eye once the six-inch-thick fleeces were removed. Several of my ewes had difficulty lambing that spring, and I became an instant convert to *scoring* my sheep (see more below) in order to keep them in optimal shape by adjusting their feed.

SCORING YOUR SHEEP

How do you know if your sheep are too fat or too thin? Short of weighing them, which would involve a host of logistical problems, there is a simple technique called *scoring*. You should score your sheep from time to time—and certainly whenever you are wondering whether you're feeding them the correct amount of hay.

Ideally, you should practice scoring your sheep in the month or two after your sheep have been shorn—when long wool won't interfere too much with your learning. If you have an experienced shepherd in the neighborhood, now is a good time to have him or her come over to help you score your sheep while you're getting the hang of it.

Run your fingers up and down the spine of your sheep from the rump to the shoulders, and also run your hand from side to side across the spine. Settle in on the lumbar spine, which is the stretch of vertebrae between the ribs and the pelvis. Each vertebra has three bony, protruding wings: one that comes straight up toward your hand, and two that stick out laterally and slightly down on each side. When you run your hands along a few vertebra and massage into the flesh, how many of these points can you feel? The answer will determine a sheep's score, on a scale from zero to five.

Score	Description
0	You can feel all three points with no hand pressure at all; in fact, you can basically see all three points because this sheep is so thin it's in imminent danger of starving to death.
1	You can feel all three points easily; the top of the spine feels sharp, and you can easily slip your fingers underneath the side points.
2	You can still feel all three points, but you can only feel under the side points by applying lots of pressure; the top point protrudes somewhat but feels smooth.
3	You can feel all three points but can't get your fingers under the side points; the top point is rounded and is even with the flesh on each side of it without protruding above.
4	You can't feel the side points at all despite good hand pressure; the top points sit down in a groove below the flesh on either side.
5	You can't feel anything; unless you knew there was a spine in there somewhere, you'd think the animal was entirely flesh.

Your sheep's score will naturally fluctuate throughout the year, with your goal being to keep every animal in the 2 to 4 range across the year. In the winter, however, you want to keep your animals in the 2+ to 3 range. If they start to get too heavy, you can cut back somewhat on the amount of hay you're feeding them or substitute some lesser quality hay.

You will undoubtedly notice variations between years and between animals. If your flock and infrastructure are extensive, you can separate your sheep into different groups based on how they score: put the too-heavies on lean rations if they bulked up too much on summer pasture, or put the too-leans on richer hay if they're lagging at a score of 2. But if you have a small flock, as I do, you will need to make decisions for the whole flock based on the average score.

I've now gone so far as to purchase an old baby scale to help me keep track of how much hay I am feeding each day, and I'd strongly advise that you do the same. Once again, the ultimate answer to whether or not you are feeding them properly comes not from a book but from running your hand along their spines and scoring them. You'd like them all to be a steady 3 or a 3 minus throughout the winter.

Finally, whatever you do, don't miss a feeding and allow your sheep to go hungry in the winter. The reason your flock can loaf around contentedly at twenty below zero is that they are burning the hay you feed them for instant heat and energy. Miss a feeding and their furnaces will go out. If you decide that your sheep are scoring too high and gaining weight over the winter, switch to lower quality hay rather than cutting off their hay altogether.

 Above: Maddie, an Oxford cross ewe, sips water from a bucket at the Mathewson home. Barbara Mathewson brings fresh water up to the sheep from the house twice a day, by hose in the summer and by bucket in the winter.

WATER

Besides pasture or hay, your sheep will need access to clean water at all times. How much they need will vary greatly over the course of the year. In the springtime, when the pastures are lush and morning dew is common, I find that my sheep require almost no supplemental water. They get everything they need from the grass. In mid-summer, when the pastures are browning and the sheep are panting from the heat, they need lots and lots of water. When autumn rains return, they once again drink less from the trough; this lasts until they go on their ration of winter hay, when they start slurping their water with renewed enthusiasm. In mid-winter, however, when I typically feed them hay directly on top of the snow, they need considerably less water since they're eating some snow along with their hay.

Regardless of how much water you are putting out for your sheep, the water needs to be clean. Sheep will avoid fetid water even when they are thirsty, so make sure there is no poop in the water or green slime or algae on the bottom. A few stems of hay floating around are fine (and, indeed, inevitable), as long as the water itself is clear and fresh. Whenever possible, locate the water trough or pails in the shade to keep the water cool and algae-free.

I find that filling a smallish water container every day or so is preferable to filling a large container infrequently: you have less of a mess on your hands when the container becomes dirty, and you can better keep track of how much your sheep are drinking and make adjustments accordingly. Most animal-supply stores sell round rubber tubs that are roughly two feet across by ten inches deep, which make ideal water troughs. They weigh very little when empty, which makes it convenient to move them around between pastures; they hold the contents of a five-gallon bucket (which, at forty pounds, is the most water I like to carry at one time); and they can freeze solid in the winter without being damaged.

You will need one of these rubber tubs for every six or so sheep, and I also keep a few extra tubs on hand to rotate in when one of the tubs starts to feel slimy inside. Letting a tub dry completely every now and again prevents any algae from growing. Setting the tubs about a foot or so off the ground will help prevent the sheep from stepping on them or pooping in the water. I've followed the lead of the friends who sold me my flock by placing my water tubs atop a stack of two old tires: they are just the right height and are not damaged by the occasional sloshing and spillage.

What about winter? In my case, where it is relatively easy to carry a bucket of fresh water from the house at feeding time, I refill the tubs at each feeding. If any excess water freezes in the tubs before the next feeding, I just knock the tubs upside down to remove the ice and make a note to bring less water next time. My sheep don't drink much water in the winter when I'm feeding them hay outside on snow, so this is a simple and low-tech solution.

High-tech solutions are available, and you may want to pursue one if your sheep shelter is far from your water supply or if you are partial to high-tech solutions. (See the tools and equipment appendix for more details.) If water already runs to your shelter, try installing a freeze-proof water trough that feeds off of a buried water line. If you have electricity to your shelter, consider installing a bubbler to slow the rate of freezing, or a heater to prevent freezing altogether. But keep in mind that a heater, while reducing your need to haul water to the barn, will greatly increase the amount of money you shovel into the electric company's envelope each month.

Whatever you do, don't adopt the old-school approach of letting your sheep wade into brooks and ponds for water. Like grazing sheep in shaded woodlands, this is a solution that seems quick and cheap in the short term; but it is actually a very expensive practice over time. Sheep standing around and pooping in water will eventually make the water too disgusting even for sheep to drink. At this point, the water will be too far gone for anything else of value—including fish and other wildlife. The ecological damage created by livestock in surface water is so extensive that at worst it is illegal; at the very least, it is contrary to the best management practices adopted by all livestock associations. So don't do it.

If you have surface water available on your land, it can still make for a quick and easy way to get water to your sheep: just set a water pail nearby

 Above: Barbara Mathewson takes a bucket of grain out of the barn to feed Bode, her Romney ram. Mathewson feeds grain to her eight sheep even in the summer—both because the grass grows thinly on her rocky pasture land and, as she says, "I'm just a softy."

that you can easily fill using a pump or buckets. How nearby is something of a tradeoff. The closer the pail is to the water source, the easier it will be to fill; the farther away the trough is, the less likely it is that sheep poop will seep through the ground and eventually reach the water. Fifty feet or so, at a minimum, is a good tradeoff.

However you decide to get water to your sheep, just make it as simple as possible. If you have to go to great lengths to keep the water clear and copious, the chances are you won't do it as often as you should—and your

sheep will suffer. Be sure to watch your sheep drink a few times. They don't lap like dogs, they slurp as if using a straw. The first time I saw this, I thought they were goofing with me and just fooling around for fun. But that's really how they drink. I find it impossible to watch an animal slurping away without breaking into some sort of chuckle.

Finally, as I mentioned earlier, you need to make sure the water is kept clean or else your sheep won't drink it. A friend of a friend of mine (stories like these are always told about a friend of a friend) was once "loaned" a flock of sheep for the summer while the regular owners were overseas. He strung up some fencing in a back pasture, put in a trough of water, and was bedeviled when the flock began to make regular escapes from the enclosure. After some weeks, they disappeared into the woods one day, never to be seen again. My friend, who was called to the scene to investigate the disappearance, was surprised to learn that his friend hadn't needed to refill the water trough all summer. "They didn't even finish the water they started with," his friend said. Putting two and two together, my friend peered into the water trough and found it grown over with algae and scum. The thirsty flock had struck out for parts unknown in search of fresh water.

MINERALS

Minerals are a year-round necessity for healthy sheep. You can buy a salt lick—a hard block of salts and minerals that your sheep will lick when they want to—or buy powdered minerals that you pour into a tray or pail. Either way, your sheep should have access to minerals whenever they want them.

Minerals act as a sort of a multi-vitamin for your sheep. Is your pasture depleted of selenium or boron, like many pastures in temperate climates? You have two options. You can fix the pasture, which means carefully measuring the amount of these trace minerals in your soil and adding soil amendments as needed; this can cost you several hundred dollars per year. Or, for roughly five dollars per sheep per year, you can give your sheep free access to minerals. If the financial savings aren't compelling enough, consider this: with the latter approach, you also have the advantage of knowing your sheep have eaten the right amount of minerals, since they've chosen them themselves.

Whether you use a salt block or powdered minerals, make sure the minerals are under some type of cover (if they are outside) so the rain won't dissolve them. Size the powdered mineral feeder so that it takes about a week for the sheep to empty it out, which is a good balance between having to fill it too often and having the uneaten minerals become hard and crusty. Roughly a quart of powdered mineral seems to keep six or eight adult sheep in minerals for a week in the winter. I find that my ewes go through the minerals much faster in the winter, when they are on dry hay, than in the summer, when they are on good pasture. Also, ewes in the final month or two of pregnancy seem to hit the minerals with renewed enthusiasm.

The only caveat for feeding minerals is to make sure you buy a mix or block intended specifically for sheep. Mineral mixes for cows or horses are higher in copper than those for sheep, which will lead to health problems for your sheep, who require less of this trace mineral than their cousins.

GRAIN

Whenever I need to be away from the farm and have someone look after my flock, they invariably ask, "What do I need to do? Feed them some grain or something?" Somehow, we've latched onto this widespread belief that barnyard animals eat grain.

By and large, they don't—and they shouldn't. It's the dairy cow and beef cow or, more specifically, our management of these animals that has created

the misconception. Farmers feed grain to dairy cows to increase their milk production, and they feed it to cattle to marble their beef with fat. But with three

Above: From left, Zion, Lily, and Jamila eat grain from a trough.

exceptions, you should avoid feeding grain to your sheep.

As I mentioned earlier, grass is what the ovine digestive tract was designed for and what keeps them healthiest year-round: pasture in summer, hay in winter. On the human end, mountains of recent research have shown that grass-fed meat is both tastier and better for us than grain-fed meat. Also, the manure from grass-fed animals is safer for us because the E.coli bacteria that live in a grass-fed gut are not the same as those that cause health problems in humans.

Then there is the financial argument: grain is expensive compared to grass. Sheep, unlike cows, do not marble their muscles with fat when fed a grain-rich diet. Instead, they store the fat separately, primarily on their hips and flanks where it does nothing but get in the way of normal lamb delivery. So the money you spend on grain doesn't improve the quality of the meat—it simply adds to the fat to be trimmed off by the butcher. Feeding grain will end up costing you money (you're selling meat, not fat) and can lead to trouble during lambing season. As a rule, don't feed grain—except for one of the following exceptions.

FEEDING GRAIN: THE EXCEPTIONS

Exception #1: Flushing

Exception #1 comes in the fall, when—if you have "bought the farm" and are raising your own lambs—you are preparing your ewes for breeding. Sheep will adjust their fertility based on the amount of food available in their environment, which is crucial to their survival in the wild. If ewes are thin and hungry in the fall, they are less likely to conceive than if they are fat and happy in the fall. Well, normal and happy. Your goal in the month leading up to breeding is to convince them that the time is right for conception by making sure your ewes are at normal weight and that the quality of their diet is improving throughout the month. This is called *flushing* the ewes, which I assume is some anthropomorphic term that associates rosy, flushed cheeks with good health. In any event, grain is the easiest way to make this happen.

Your goal during flushing is twofold: to have your ewes score a 3 to 3+ while the ram is visiting and to expose your ewes to an ever-increasing level of nutrition during his visit. If you do this, you'll likely be rewarded with twins all around come spring. The general strategy is to ramp up the ewes with extra hay and some grain for the three weeks before the ram arrives, keep them on a full ration while the ram is in residence, and then taper off the grain for the three weeks after he leaves.

Score your ewes first to decide what a full ration ought to be. A pound or two of grain per animal per day is great if they're underweight; a quarter to half that amount is sufficient if they're already getting plump; simply feeding extra second-cut hay may be fine if your ewes already score 3+ at the start of breeding season. Whatever you decide, make sure you make the change slowly. Start with just a few mouthfuls of grain per day for the first day or so. Then work up to a full serving over the course of a week, giving the grain-digesting microbes in the animals time to reproduce enough to handle the new load.

Exception #2: Lambing

Although the gestation time for a lamb is approximately five months (148 days, on average), most of a lamb's growth happens in the final two months. From the wild ewe's perspective, this makes good sense: get bred in the fall after (hopefully) a summer of good feeding, keep the fetus as small as possible during the lean winter months, and have the lamb grow rapidly just before it's due to be born in the spring—and just as spring's bounty of grass emerges.

Feeding grain to a ewe all winter won't help the lamb size up at all, but it can make the ewe too fat. In the last four to six weeks of gestation, however, the ewe can use the extra nutrition to help the lamb size up. Once again, score your ewes before deciding whether to give them supplemental grain. If your flock is already averaging a score of a solid 3 or above, stay with straight hay. If you have a bunch that score 2 or below, start them on grain immediately: sheep will abort a fetus during the winter if their rations are so thin that their biological wisdom decides a lamb won't survive in the spring. As with flushing, a pound or two of grain per animal per day is a hefty ration.

Exception #3: Lactation

Once the lambs are born, your ewes will put lots of energy into making milk for their lambs. At this point, perhaps more than at any other time of

 Above: Bijou, a twelve-year-old Romney ewe, is one of John O'Brien's movie-star sheep. As the director of a triology of films set in his hometown in Vermont, O'Brien has used grain to choreograph his flock on film--whether it's following a character through a scene or posing under a marquee to promote his latest film.

the year, their health (and the health of their lambs) will be improved with supplemental grain, especially if it's still too early in the spring for the ewes to be out grazing on fresh pasture. A pound or two of grain per animal per day can make a world of difference.

But don't overdo it: you don't want your ewes producing more milk than their lambs can drink. This can lead to *mastitis*, an inflammation of the udder that you very much want to avoid. Keep an eye on the ewes and adjust their grain accordingly. Once the lambs start eating solid food of their own—which is typically after three to four weeks of life—reduce the grain and then stop feeding grain to the mothers. This will reduce their milk production and start the natural process of weaning the lambs.

Just before giving birth to lambs in the spring, each of your ewes should ideally be a 3+: having plenty of muscle and fat reserves without having so much fat as to obscure the birth canal. After giving birth and lactating for a few months, those same ewes will have lost weight and will be down around 2. After weaning the lambs and eating good pasture all summer, they should be back to 3. Flushing during breeding may bring them back as high as 4 by late fall. The lean hay rations of winter will bring them back down to 3, before the final pre-birth grain feeding begins to bring them up to 3+. That's the ideal cycle.

Exception #4: Crowd Control

OK, there actually is a fourth exception to the no-grain rule—but it's a psychological exception, not a nutritional exception. Sheep will go almost anywhere and do almost anything if they believe there will be grain waiting for them when they get there. Your life as a shepherd will be greatly improved by making judicious use of this fact. Whereas before you were trying (in vain) to somehow herd your sheep through gates and between pens; now, with grain in the offing, your sheep will follow on your heel as obediently as the loyal family pooch.

The crucial consideration is this: it isn't the grain that motivates your sheep, it's the belief that grain is imminent. Whenever you are feeding grain to your sheep for one of the previous three exceptions, make sure you take the opportunity to condition them to the fact that grain is coming. I swirl the grain around a few times in the big coffee can that I use for dispensing grain before I actually dump it into the feeder, which causes the sheep to circle like piranhas in anticipation (if herbivores can be said to circle like piranhas) and occasionally causes one of my full-grown ewes to leap in the air like a lamb.

As a result, I can now walk out into any pasture, swirl a little grain around in a coffee can, and lead my sheep around as if they were leashed. Two summers ago, a strong thunderstorm at night blew a tree down across the fence where my lambs were pastured during weaning. The lambs flew the coop, as it were, and turned up the next morning under a tree in my neighbor's backyard, about a quarter mile away. I grabbed a coffee can of grain and coolly led them up the road and back to the barn. (OK, it wasn't quite that splendid; the lambs weren't as accustomed to the grain trick as their mothers,

Above: Paula, a Romney ewe, grazes at Landgoes Farm.

so a friend of mine took our dog on a leash to help round up the stragglers.)

Last year, I inadvertently took the grain trick to a new level. My sheep like to baa with enthusiasm and anticipation whenever I'm feeding them grain, so I took to baaing right back at them, with equal enthusiasm, as I swirled the grain in the coffee can. (You'll find that your life takes interesting turns as a shepherd.) In any event, I soon discovered they had come to associate my baaing with an impending ration of grain. Now I have only to walk among the sheep and let out a few "baas" to have them line up behind me and follow me around. I don't even need the grain anymore.

Best of all, this has caused visitors to our farm to believe I have some sort of supernatural power over sheep. They watch in amazement from the kitchen window as my sheep jump up from idle loafing, line up by rank and serial number, and follow me around like a string of kindergarteners holding onto a rope. This delights me every time I need to move my flock, and I rarely bother to inform my guests how I pulled it off.

But there are two caveats. First, you really should make a point of giving grain to your sheep after they've performed this trick for you, both out of ethical probity and your need to have them perform it again next time without doubt or reservation. Second, don't give them much grain when you do this, and don't do it too often. Otherwise, you'll effectively be raising grain-fed animals, which you should avoid for the financial and health considerations I mentioned earlier.

Grain Feeder Design

For the times when you want to feed grain to your flock, you'll need some sort of feeder to hold the grain. You can buy plastic troughs that sit on the ground, which is an easy if somewhat expensive solution. Your sheep will end up stepping in the trough, however, so you'll have to brush the feeder clean between servings. I use my hay feeder for grain as well; I throw the grain onto the bottom shelf and then slide the hay down into the rack above. If you don't want to use your hay feeder, almost anything that keeps the grain contained and off the ground will work for a feeder. Friends of mine nailed a few boards, at roughly sheep-head height, between the studs of their shelter wall and left it at that.

CHANGING DIETS

Finally, as I stressed at the outset, the key to the proper care and feeding of your sheep is to make no sudden moves. If it's time to start feeding grain to the ewes before lambing time, work them up to a full ration over the course of a week, and do the same when taking them off it later. If you buy some new hay that's full of alfalfa and clover, work it into the mix slowly and don't just toss it into the all-you-can-eat buffet. Finally, when it's time to turn your sheep into pasture in the springtime, fill their bellies full of dry hay first, and then give them only an hour or so in the pasture per day for the first few days. Gradually work them up to full pasture over the course of a week or so, and keep feeding them dry hay during that time.

The danger of going to a too-rich, too-soon diet is that your sheep will develop bloat. They won't yet have sufficient rich-diet bacteria in their rumens to break down the sudden abundance, and the food will rot, ferment, emit gas, and—in the extreme case— cause the sheep to explode. (Well, that's somewhat on the dramatic side; their expanding digestive tract will probably squeeze their lungs and suffocate them before they actually explode. But you get the idea.)

The flip side is also a danger: the too-poor, too-soon diet. If you realize one day that your sheep are overweight and decide to drastically reduce their rations, they will adjust by digging into their fat reserves and burning fat for energy, too much of which can overwhelm their livers and lead to toxemia. Your sheep will become lethargic, listless, and stupefied before keeling over dead. More or less. So always reduce rations slowly so that the fat comes off over time instead of all at once.

Though the dangers here sound extreme (and they are extreme), they are easily avoided. Don't worry. Just make sure that you phase in all diet changes over the course of a few weeks or so. Once their rumens have adapted to the new regimen, they'll be fine, and so will you.

If your sheep are anything like my sheep, they will be quick to let you know when you've made a mistake and screwed up their food. Pay attention to them, especially if they start acting different than they usually do. My sheep rarely make any noise at all, unless I'm egging them on with grain. If I hear them baaing from the barnyard only an hour or two after I've fed them, I can be sure that something is wrong that needs correcting. Take the time to figure out what's going on. If proper shepherding could be boiled down to a single, over-simplified sentence, it would be this: get the diet right, and everything else will take care of itself.

One final story about my sheep at feeding time. Early in our first winter together, as the sheep became attuned to my dawn-and-dusk feeding schedule, they would start baaing for me each morning just as the sun began breaking the horizon. Shortly thereafter, the sheep noticed that their dawn feeding was always preceded by a light being turned on inside the farmhouse, which was me moving about, firing the woodstove up, and looking for my jacket and boots. Now they began baaing for me as soon as they saw a light turn on. Eager to stay in my sleeping wife's good graces, I countered by lighting the woodstove in the dark so that the sheep wouldn't yet know I was awake. But the sheep, not to be outdone, noticed that my awakening was always preceded by the automatic timer turning on the oil furnace in the basement, with the furnace's attendant plume of smoke and steam rising from the chimney above the house. Now the timer starts the furnace, the furnace wakes the sheep, the sheep wake me, and none of us needs an alarm clock anymore. Who said sheep were dumb?

CHAPTER FIVE

Fencing

Unless you have a couple of hundred acres of open prairie and a pack of sheep dogs at your command, you're going to need some fencing to separate your sheep from the wider world.

Good fencing is a joy to behold. It's attractive and effective. It gently guides your sheep by offering reasonable directives that they are happy to follow. And it affords you great delight whenever, with the simple flick of a gate latch, you move your flock from one pasture to another.

Bad fencing, on the other hand, is none of these things. It looks like hell. It's temperamental and unreliable—often scaring the flock and causing them to do things they don't want to do. Inevitably, when you attempt to move your flock from one pasture to another with the aforementioned flick of a latch gate, bad fencing will suck a half-day's worth of frustrated effort out of you.

The main difference between good fencing and bad fencing is that good fencing is designed in advance to handle every circumstance, both the likely and the unlikely. Bad fencing, on the other hand, is designed only for the average or best-case scenario. Bad fencing works just fine until you really need it most. Then it doesn't.

Fortunately, good fencing requires no more effort to install and maintain than bad fencing: you just need to put in that time and effort up front. This, of course, is something that I did not do

Opposite: Lambs peek at a visitor to Barbara Mathewson's farm. Mathewson and her husband Bob set up the woven wire fence when they bought the house and land in the early 1980s. She prefers working with non-electrified fence.

 Above: Nan, a Border collie, keeps an eye on her flock of twenty-two charges as they graze across a town green in Vermont. The dog later moved the flock two miles up the road to owner Steve Wetmore's farm.

before I arrived home with our first flock. With the benefit of hindsight, however, and in order to make this chapter on fencing go as smoothly as possible, I have developed a "four concentric circle" theory of sheep fencing to help explain the basics. Each of the four circles is designed to handle a specific task and make that task go as easily as possible for the shepherd and the flock.

But before delving further into this revolutionary theory of optimized, concentric-circle sheep fencing, a word about electricity.

ELECTRIC VERSUS NON-ELECTRIC FENCING

Some shepherds electrify nearly all of the fencing on their farms. Others go an entirely non-electric route. Still others, like me, use a combination of

the two. Each approach has distinct advantages and disadvantages that are worth considering in advance.

The simplest is the non-electric route. The advantages of having all non-electric fencing are quite obvious: you don't need to mess with chargers and insulators and associated accoutrements, and you never have to worry about whether you or an unsuspecting friend of yours (or their child) will accidentally lean against a hot wire. Plus, with a non-electric fence, you can tell at a glance whether or not the fence is working: if it's standing, it's working. There's never the nagging question—after the thunderstorm or the heavy dew or the fallen branch or the deep snow—of whether the thing shorted out or something.

The disadvantage of the non-electric fence is that it quickly becomes more expensive and difficult to install than electric fence. If you're running three sheep in your backyard to keep the weeds down, no big deal: driving a few extra posts for their enclosure is cheaper than buying an electric charger. But if you have as few as a half-dozen sheep on your spread, you'll find that the economic balance rapidly starts to tip in favor of electrification as the amount of fencing you need increases.

Electric fence's advantages and disadvantages are, as you'd imagine, just the opposite: electric is usually cheaper and easier to install, and it's much easier to take down and move if you decide you'd rather rework your fencing after a few years of experience. On the downside, you can guarantee that friends, kids, dogs, and hapless passersby are going to be zapped every now and again—and that goes for you too. Also, electric fencing needs to be on 100% of the time; if your flock becomes accustomed to electric fencing during periods when it's not on, they will be quick to push through it later on, even when the juice is restored.

Getting shocked isn't the end of the world. It just feels like it. Fence chargers have been carefully designed over the years to inflict an amazing amount of pain without causing any actual harm. Last year I made it into August before being zapped by my fence, which was a personal record. I usually turn the charger on for the season around May 1—and typically receive my first inadvertent thwack by month's end.

From your flock's perspective, non-electric fencing is a physical barrier, while electric fencing is a pain barrier. This is a key distinction. Sheep can't get through a physical barrier regardless of how badly they want to (assuming the fence is strong and tall). With a pain barrier, however, the sheep may decide they want to get through it even more than they want to avoid the shock (when a dog is chasing them, for example), and so they will break through. If the result of your sheep escaping is they end up taking a dip in your pond or gaining access to fresh pasture before you want them to, that's not too bad a risk to take. But if they end up eating your prize-winning pumpkins or dashing onto the median of an interstate highway, you might want to reconsider the risk. If it's essential that your sheep not escape through a certain section of fence, then that section needs to be non-electric.

Most shepherds end up using a combination of fencing types: non-electric where they really need it to work all the time and electric where the occasional lapse is neither likely nor apocalyptic. That's the approach I've been using, and one I would highly recommend.

With that electrifying discussion out of the way, back to the four concentric circles of fencing: the confinement pen, the shelter pen, the barnyard, and the perimeter fence.

CIRCLE #1: THE CONFINEMENT PEN

The confinement pen is, quite simply, a pen designed to be so small that when you herd your flock into it, the animals are crowded cheek by jowl and have enough space to stand up but not move around. Veteran shepherds often refer to this as a forcing pen or crowding pen. There will be several key times over the course of a year when you will want to handle and inspect your sheep—perhaps to trim a hoof, check an udder, or sell a lamb or two to your neighbor. You'll want to be able to work with individual animals without having to chase them around and cut them out of the flock. Having a confinement pen makes this simple and easy. Not having one leads to a game of keep-away that typically ends when the shepherd either sprains a wrist or gives up.

The simplest way to create a confinement pen is to hang a gate inside your shelter, near a corner. When you want to confine the flock, simply work them into the corner (a can of grain usually provides ample motivation) and pull the gate out from the wall to close them in. This works brilliantly when you tend to have the same number of sheep from year to year so that the gate always closes to the right size.

If your flock fluctuates in size throughout the year as lambs come and go, you can either make a fence panel (see the tools and supplies appendix for details) or use a gate that is off its hinges to push your flock into the corner. Then lash the panel or gate to the walls to keep it secured at the right size.

No matter how you decide to build your confinement pen, it's best if you construct it inside your shelter pen (the second concentric circle of fencing) as opposed to outside somewhere. Administering vaccines and trimming hooves is sufficiently exciting on its own without the addition of standing in the rain and grappling oily sheep.

In the ideal world, most or all of the walls of your confinement pen should be solid so your sheep can't see through them. You might think that the sheep would like to see what is going on around them when they're in the confinement pen, but that would be the predator in you making that assumption. Remember the huddle that scared sheep will create, with their eyes inside and their tails outside? You want your confinement pen to recreate these conditions. Your sheep would rather not watch the shearer set up the equipment or watch you load up the vaccination needle. They'd rather have the security of a nice, solid wall.

Novice shepherds often believe they can do without a confinement pen because it seems somehow cruel to force their sheep into a corner with scarcely enough room to breathe. But remember that being separated from the flock is the number one hazard that sheep will go to extraordinary lengths to avoid. When I work with my flock inside the confinement pen, the animals often seem downright happy to have me in there, ministering to their needs and discomforts while they remain in physical contact with their companions.

Every now and then, however, when I just want to sneak a look at one particular sheep for a moment or two, I'll try to take it by surprise and catch it out in the open. On the rare occasion when I'm successful, the sheep will squirm and wriggle and give me such a look of loathing that I'll have neither the heart nor the strength to do whatever it was that I set out to do. Usually, I herd the entire flock into the confinement pen even when I just want to look at one animal. The flock knows the drill at this point, and they dutifully allow me to crowd them in and confine them temporarily without so much as a baa of complaint.

However you decide to construct your confinement pen, it should not be electrified! Both you and your sheep will be pressing directly against it as you go about your shepherding chores, so make the pen good and sturdy—but don't plug it in. Make it as easy as possible for you to use this pen. If it's easy, you won't hesitate to confine your flock whenever you want to, and your sheep will get used to the process. If it's difficult, you won't use the pen as often as you should, and your flock (and you) will suffer.

CIRCLE #2: FENCING AROUND THE SHELTER

The next concentric circle of fencing is the fencing (or walls) around your shelter. Though you'll want your sheep to have free-choice access to the outdoors whenever possible (sheep just aren't fully sheep when they're penned up indoors for long periods), there are also times when you'll want them confined to their shelter: for example, when you want to keep them dry before shearing or keep the ewes in at night during lambing season. For these tasks, you'll want to be able to fence your flock inside out of the weather.

Your shelter fence is also a classic spot where you'll want a physical barrier, not a pain barrier—one that always works and can be relied upon with 100% certainty. If your shelter is a barn or shed with wooden walls, so

much the better. Install a gate or door to go with them, and you're done. If you'll be building walls for an otherwise open-sided shelter, make them four to five feet tall. This will prevent excited sheep from jumping out and keep unwanted canines from jumping in, which is the more likely of the two to occur. You want to know your flock is safe and secure when confined to their shelter, no matter the circumstances.

The pen we have in our barn has solid wooden walls on two sides (the barn walls

 Above: Marian White gives her Navajo-Churro flock a snack in the barnyard. This fence is high and tight to keep predators out as the snow pack deepens through the winter.

 Above: Bode, a Romney ram, peers through woven wire fence. Owner Barbara Mathewson said her sheep will lean against the fence to weaken it and try to crawl underneath if they're after grass on the other side.

themselves) and wooden boards about four feet high on the other two sides. This serves as a nice combination: we are able to see in over the half walls and the sheep have the confidence and security of the two full-sized walls whenever they decide there is too much action and commotion coming from our side. Plus, they love the wooden walls for rubbing against, something they could not do if this shelter fence were electrified.

A few more words about sheep psychology are in order here: sheep will tend to avoid shadows, dark spaces, sharp contrasts between light and dark, and places they can't see into. You want your shelter fencing, therefore, to create the opposite conditions so that your flock will never hesitate to go inside when needed. Good shelter fencing is a combination of being completely solid (like walls) to provide a feeling of security and wide open (like regular fencing) to allow for good visibility. Solid wooden fencing on either two or three sides of the shelter with open wire fencing on the other one or two sides seems like the ideal arrangement, because the sheep have a nice mix of security and light.

In my first attempt at shelter fencing, I built a slatted wall on one side of our pen because it took less scrap wood to make than a solid wall. But over several years, I noticed that the slatted wall seemed to bother the sheep: they could see through it enough to sense movement and activity but not enough to have a full view of what was going on. I've since rounded up more scrap wood and made the wall solid.

Sheep will shy away from anything that moves. One breezy spring afternoon, a friend of mine who had spun and woven a rug using the wool from our sheep came by the farm to take a picture of the sheep grazing contentedly in front of "their" rug. We hung the rug over a fence, where it flapped gently in the wind, and waited for the sheep to get near enough for a photo. They didn't. Instead, they went to the opposite side of the pasture. We moved the rug closer to them; they moved farther away from it. We have a few photos of big sheep in the foreground and a tiny rug in the distance, but not the photo we had intended to get.

Armed with this new knowledge, I noticed several old tarps I had stacked on our barn floor near the door to the sheep pen, which would blow around when big gusts of wind hit the barn. I also noticed that the sheep always turned to look at the tarps whenever this happened, which was a needless annoyance for them. So I moved the tarps elsewhere. You would do well to also take a moment to view your shelter area from an ovine perspective. Do your best to minimize things that move, are dark, are hard to see, or that cause unnecessary stress.

CIRCLE #3: THE BARNYARD

Sheep coming and going from their shelter will trample the grass near the door and poop on it. Sheep will also loaf around right outside the shelter, because they like knowing they can duck inside to safety if needed. Both of these activities will either stunt, kill, or render inedible all the grass growing in the vicinity. Your job is to minimize this damage by fencing in a "barnyard" immediately adjacent to the shelter. This is the third concentric circle of fencing.

A good barnyard is roughly two to three times larger than the shelter space itself, which gives the flock plenty of room to move around. Figure on roughly twenty square feet of barnyard per animal. Within a year or two, nearly all of the grass in this area will be gone, and you'll have a classic dirt barnyard on your hands. Make sure, therefore, that the barnyard isn't on low ground that will stay soggy after rain and snow. If it is, bring in some sand or gravel so your sheep can stay high and dry. Or better yet, put the barnyard somewhere else. Hooves that are chronically wet and caked with mud will eventually cause their owners (and you) lots of distress.

The idea behind the barnyard is that it gives your flock constant access to the outdoors. There will be times (such as winter and early spring) when you'll want to keep your sheep off your pastures but don't want to lock them up inside the shelter. That's when the barnyard is ideal: the flock can come and go at will without having access to the wider world.

Most shepherds enclose the barnyard with a standard sheep fencing called *woven wire*, which is a metal mesh that's not electrified. If you plan to have lambs in your flock, or rams (or even ewes) with horns, use woven wire that has vertical wires spaced every three inches so the lambs can't escape through the holes and the adults can't inadvertently get their heads stuck. Woven wire usually comes with either three-inch, six-inch, or twelve-inch spacing of the vertical wires, but three is best for the barnyard fence. I didn't know this when I installed my first woven wire, so I bought what the local feed store had for sale, which was six-inch. Each spring, my ewes poke their heads through the six-inch openings to get at the fresh grass on the far side. This works out fine because none of my ewes have horns. If they did, the six-inch openings would work just like lobster pots, and I'd spend each afternoon freeing hapless horned heads. Besides being an annoyance, this can be positively dangerous for the sheep—especially if they get stuck in the sun on a hot day and panic.

Some shepherds opt to run a strand or two of electrified wire along the posts above the woven wire, primarily as a deterrent against the canine crowd in the winter. This may not seem obvious when you install your fence in the summer; but several feet of snow with a crust on top will turn your formidable four-foot-high barrier into a minor two-foot-high obstacle that hungry coyotes or rowdy dogs will hurdle without a second thought. I have yet to install these hot wires at our place, but it seems well worth doing if you regularly see that kind of winter (or that kind of canine).

At some point you will consider using barbed wire for your sheep fencing, since it is both readily available and relatively inexpensive. Avoid this temptation! Barbed wire is great for short-haired ungulates like cows and horses, but it is disastrous for their wooly cousins. A sheep's wool is usually thick enough to prevent the barbs from reaching the skin and deterring the animal, who will push against the fence with enthusiasm. Even if the sheep don't push through your barbed wire fence altogether, the barbs will tear off nice chunks of wool—to the detriment of the sheep and your wool sales.

The gates that lead out of your barnyard need to be strong enough to resist regular ovine investigation, yet easy to open and close. Because the barnyard will serve as your central grazing hub, with access to various pasture areas, you'll be using these gates frequently. The hole spacing on whatever gates you decide to buy or make also matters, and the three-inch rule applies here too. Whether I buy a prefabricated metal gate or make my own out of wood, I usually lash a section of woven wire to each one. The metal gates that are readily available in our area are designed for horses or dairy cows; without the addition of woven wire, the spaces are big enough for even adult sheep to step through.

Finally, put in your best effort installing the barnyard fence. Your sheep will be up against it more than any other fence and will, without a doubt, find any holes and weak spots. If a sheep escapes, the whole flock will become distraught once the escapee discovers his or her error and tries valiantly to get back in. It takes a lot of grain and determination to convince a wayward sheep to follow you along the fence, usually away from the cries of the waiting flock, to the nearest gate for readmittance. Rather than letting loose a string of "!@# sheep!" epithets as you try to convince the lost sheep to abandon its instinctive desire to stay close to the herd, try "!@# shepherd!" instead. It wasn't the sheep who installed the fence.

CIRCLE #4: THE PERIMETER

The fourth and largest concentric circle of fencing for you to consider is the outermost perimeter of your proposed grazing area. Whether you intend to rotate your sheep among many pastures or simply turn them out in a single, large field for the summer, you'll need a fence that goes around the outside of everything.

Here's where electrified fence really comes into its own, because it's much quicker and cheaper to install long runs of electric fence than woven wire. Instead of wooden posts installed every ten feet or so to support the woven wire, a high-tensile electric fence requires strong posts only at the corners. The fence wires—usually five feet high for sheep—are pulled tightly between these corners, with only lightweight spacers required along the fence itself to prevent the wires from sagging.

A second advantage of having an electric perimeter fence is that it makes it easy to use portable electric netting to subdivide large pastures for rotational grazing. Netting comes in long roles that you simply unroll where you want it, push in the support posts, and attach it to the electric perimeter fence to electrify it. When it's time to move it, you simply reverse the process and take the netting over to the new location. A 164-foot roll of netting can be taken down, moved, and put back up in only five minutes or so.

Suddenly you see how easy it can be to set up a system for rotating your sheep between pastures for optimal grazing efficiency: put a high-tensile electric fence around the perimeter and use portable netting to subdivide individual pastures inside as needed.

It can be even easier than that. At our farm—where sheep coexist with a retail vegetable operation and where both the sheep and the vegetables seem to be multiplying each year—I haven't had a good idea of where our permanent perimeter fence ought to be

 Above: Roker, a three-year-old Black Welsh Mountain ram, grazes near portable netting that owner Linda Doane uses to rotationally graze her flock at Maple Ridge Sheep Farm.

placed. What is pasture now might be vegetables next year, and if our flock keeps growing, they may need a new shelter in the future that's closer to the main pasture. So I've skipped the permanent perimeter fence altogether, and I simply run rolls of netting out from the gates of the barnyard, with a central fence charger providing the juice.

But then there are those shepherds who use woven wire for all the fencing on their farm, including the perimeter fence and any inside pasture subdivisions. It seems that a more complete discussion of the pros and cons of each of these three fencing options (high-tensile electric, electric netting, and woven wire) is in order.

THE PERMANENT ELECTRIC PERIMETER: HIGH-TENSILE FENCE

As I mentioned earlier, the advantages of using high-tensile, electric fencing are that it's the cheapest option to buy, it's the easiest permanent fencing to install, and it can be used to feed electricity to portable netting. In addition, because the wires are held under tension by springs, the wires can withstand being hit by a falling tree or limb and still bounce back with minimal damage. If your fencing is going to run along a tree line or near the edge of a woods, this is something to keep in mind: a year doesn't go by when at least one tree or limb doesn't fall out of the woods onto our eight-acre pasture.

The two main disadvantages of the high-tensile electric fence both stem from its being electrified: it can shock people and passersby just as easily as it can sheep, and it can become completely ineffective if it is shorted out, especially by weeds growing up into it. Electric fence, therefore, requires regular maintenance during the grass-growing season: at the very least, an occasional pass with a mower or weed whacker to keep the weeds and grass from reaching the wires. If you already own a tractor or mower or weed whacker, this may be a minor burden. But if you don't, it's an expense that starts to make the high-tensile option seem not quite so inexpensive.

Installing gates in a high-tensile fence is relatively straightforward. Either use a metal or wood gate, as you did for the barnyard; or, if it's a gate

that you will only need to open every now and then, put in a spring-coil gate. A spring-coil gate consists of five (usually) slinky-like springs that stretch across the opening and are electrified by the fence when they're closed. While not as convenient to open and close as a regular gate, they are cheaper to install and, because they are electrified just like the fence, may be a better predator deterrent than a "cold" metal or wood gate.

 Above: A lamb walks along a woven wire fence on the Mathewson property. All fencing will sag over time. While this fence still works to guide sheep between pastures, it wouldn't be strong enough for the barnyard.

 Above: A radio hangs from a tree in the pasture at Landgoes Farm. All-night talk-radio can be effective at keeping predators away from the flock.

THE PORTABLE ELECTRIC PERIMETER: NETTING

Portable netting is even more susceptible to being shorted out by weeds than high-tensile fencing, for the simple reason that there's lots more wire in a net that the weeds can easily reach. Netting is the most expensive per foot of the three perimeter options. Also, you need to consider the fact that netting needs to be moved on a regular basis, either to bring your flock to new grass or to get the netting away from the weeds. If you start talking acres and acres of pasture, this could add up to several hours of labor per week.

Finally, netting needs to be electrified 100% of the time when it's in use. Your sheep will lose their fear of netting if it's not turned on and will learn to press and graze against it. If they should become tangled in it later on when it's electrified—especially an unknowing ram lamb with budding horns—the result will be somewhere between terrifying and fatal.

But there are also distinct advantages of netting. First of all, instead of trying to mow the weeds underneath it as you would with high-tensile fencing, you simply move the netting to a new area that you mowed in advance. (Wait, you ask—aren't the sheep supposed to be doing the mowing? Yes, but when a lush pasture meets the boot-top test and is ready for grazing, the grass will be tall enough to affect the portable netting. Mowing a stripe in which to put the fence minimizes the shorting out.)

Second, netting is infinitely flexible. Do you want your flock to graze that slope up above your driveway that's too steep for a tractor? Put some netting around it and they're ready to go. Do you want to convert that section of lawn to pasture? Or that pasture to garden? Or your neighbor's field into a pasture for late summer? With netting, it's easily done—as is changing your mind next year and doing it a different way.

Third, you don't have to worry about gates and how people are going to get around the fencing; just turn off the charger and step over the fence. Our pasture area is a popular ski and snow-machine area in the winter, and a popular deer and turkey hunting spot in the spring and fall. But it's no problem, for the netting is down at those times. In fact, as soon as the sheep return to the barnyard for the winter once the grass runs out, I take down all the netting and mow the whole pasture to prevent undesirable plants from taking over. With no fencing and gates to worry about, this is an easy task.

The Non-Electric Perimeter: Woven Wire

If you don't want to worry about weeds and fence chargers and zapped children, and if you want to be able to tell from afar whether or not your fence is working, then a woven wire perimeter may be for you. Woven wire is also the best choice if the results of your sheep escaping would be catastrophic, such as eating the neighbor's prized perennial patch or wandering out onto a busy highway.

There are two ways to install woven wire: the way I did it my first time, and the right way. I used a post-hole digger to install cedar posts, rolled the fencing out along the posts, and then lifted it up and nailed it on. Now, several years later, the posts are wobbly, the fence sags, and there are numerous places where my sheep can "shoulder" under the fence in pursuit of choice morsels on the far side. Perhaps this is why I'm not a big fan of woven wire.

The right way is to drive the posts into the ground, not dig them in, and then stretch the woven wire tightly between the posts (especially along the bottom of the fence, where the sheep will press against it) before nailing it on. In fact, I've seen woven wire referred to as *high-tensile woven wire*—an excellent concept that bears no resemblance to what I installed. I've seen these fences done right at other farms, and they are a beauty to behold.

The main advantage of woven wire is that, if you're willing to put in the time and money up front to do it right, and if you're sure you know where you think the perimeter fence ought to be, then you do it once and you're done. Regardless of the weather or the weeds or the snow, your fence is working. As I mentioned before, I've also seen people run a few strands of electrified wire on the posts above the woven wire to cover the coyote-on-a-crust case from mid-winter.

The two main disadvantages of a woven wire perimeter fence, besides the up-front expense and the difficulty of changing your mind later, are the fallen tree and the difficulty of using netting to subdivide pastures. If a tree or limb falls and breaks the woven wire, you'll have to fix that section of fence, and fix it in such a way that you haven't lost all the tension that prevents it from sagging and bagging. And if you want to use electrified netting inside the perimeter, you'll need to get the electricity supplied from somewhere besides the fence itself, and you'll have to make darned sure that the netting doesn't lean against the woven wire. Weeds don't short out netting nearly as well as woven wire.

There are two options for installing gates in a woven wire fence. If you're going to be using the gate frequently, a metal or wooden gate is the way to go. But if you'll only need to open the gate once or twice per year, say to get a tractor in for mowing, consider making a gate out of the woven wire itself. Install your fence posts per usual, which is one every ten feet. Where you want the gate to be, set a second "dummy" post on the ground next to the permanent post you've driven into the ground. Run the woven wire fencing up to the dummy post and staple it on. Then, use wire (or specially designed metal horseshoe-shaped brackets) to lash the dummy post next to the permanent post. When it's time to open the gate, undo the lashings and pull the fence open. It's a simple way to have a gate without going to all the trouble and expense of installing a true gate.

FENCING: IF I HAD TO DO IT OVER AGAIN

If I had to do over again—and I knew everything then that I know now and had the money to do it all up front—here are the choices I'd make in laying out my four concentric circles of fencing.

I'd use wood for the walls of the shelter and the confinement pen; there's something wonderful about working with wood, and the sheep love it for rubbing and security. I'd use woven wire for the barnyard, with no electrified wires on top unless I really had a canine problem. I'd choose high-tensile electric fence for the perimeter, because it's not the end of the world if my sheep escape into the woods every now and then, and I could use the electricity for feeding the netting subdivision inside. With a few key gates and removable netting inside, I could still mow the place pretty easily.

PREDATORS

If the main goal of fencing is to keep your sheep in, a critical secondary role of fencing is to keep predators out. The main predators of sheep are the canine crowd—dogs, coyotes, wolves, and foxes—with coyotes alone responsible for more than half of all predator-related sheep deaths in the United States each year. Bears have also been known to kill sheep on occasion, as have mountain lions and bobcats. Your job as a shepherd is to assess how much danger predators pose to your flock and act accordingly. I am pleased to report that, although our farm is regularly visited by dogs, coyotes, and foxes, we have yet to lose a single animal to predation.

First and foremost, you need to view your operation through the eyes of an opportunistic coyote. Are tasty young lambs grazing far away from their shelter and their parents, especially in the fall when wild food is becoming scarce? Step right up! Or would I, as a coyote, have to cross several fences and pass by the shepherd's house each night, only to find that the lambs are safely inside the barn in the company of their parents? I suspect I'd go elsewhere for less risky fare.

Your sheep are most at risk of predation when they are far from their shelter, at night, in the winter. They are least at risk when they are inside during the day in the summer. I freely leave our flock outside in distant pastures during the summer months but would never do that in the late autumn and winter when our local coyotes are often going to sleep hungry.

Your second line of defense is electricity, a newfangled technology that canines don't (yet) understand. As you can imagine, portable electric netting is an extremely effective predator deterrent because its holes are too small for penetration and its sting is too painful to warrant further investigation. A strand or two of high-tensile electric atop or adjacent to a wooden or woven-wire fence can also go a long way toward preventing a predator from figuring out how to gain access. Lights and radios can give the impression of more human activity than a predator wants to take on. Try installing a floodlight outside the shelter door that will illuminate the barnyard while still allowing the sheep to sleep inside in the dark, or hook up an old radio inside the shelter and tune it to an all-night, talk-radio station. Those all-night, talk-radio shows can deter all sorts of critters.

If you have a serious predator problem on your hands, then you should consider adding a guard animal to your flock. Donkeys and llamas are great choices, because they instinctively turn to face and confront potential predators. With all but the most desperate attackers, the threat of resistance is more important than resistance itself. A local shepherd I know has a llama in with her flock, and when my wife and I stopped by for a visit, the llama immediately rounded up the flock, herded them into a corner, and stood between us and the sheep, waving her head menacingly and stomping her hooves at us. This performance was quite impressive from where we stood, and I can only assume that it would be that much more so from the canine vantage point.

Opposite: Chuck the llama handles security for a Navajo-Churro flock. Llamas are effective guards because they're taller than sheep, look around while chewing their food, and round up the flock when they sense danger.

Another option is to raise or buy a guard dog that will live with your sheep. This will not be a family pet but rather a dog that's been raised to think it is a sheep and will rise to the defense of the flock in a pinch. Keep in mind that keeping any guard animal will lead to a certain amount of expense and effort on your part. If you are protecting a large flock from a known threat, this expense will be quickly repaid. If you're protecting a small flock from a hypothetical threat (you have coyotes in your neighborhood, none of which have ever caused you any trouble), you'll find that closing the barn door at night is a much more practical solution.

Of all the anti-predator strategies out there, shooting the offenders is among the easiest yet least effective roads to take. For starters, shooting, poisoning, or snaring wild animals is often either illegal or involves visits from the game warden and other authorities. More important, however, is the simple biological fact that canine fertility is linked to food supply, not adult mortality. Shooting a few coyotes in the fall will simply ensure that more pups are born the following spring to take up the chase. Your life as a shepherd will pass far more pleasantly if you make use of fences, electricity, and guard animals to deter predators than if you spend a string of nights out in the far pastures trying to stay awake with a rifle in your lap.

FINAL THOUGHTS ON FENCING

Don't be too intimidated! You're going to make changes and adjustments to your fencing system as you become a more experienced shepherd, so don't feel that you have to get everything 100% correct at the outset. A little planning in the beginning will help you avoid having to replace and redo everything a few years down the road; but no amount of planning at the outset will insulate you from having to make some modifications at some point. Your goal isn't perfection, it's doing your best. You can always go for perfection later on.

And when you go for perfection, you might decide to hire professionals to do the job. Check the yellow pages under *fencing*. It didn't occur to me at the start of my shepherding career that I could hire people who knew something about fencing; I assumed that I had to do it myself. While I don't regret the adventures and misadventures I've had to date while wielding fencing tools, I do believe I'll go with the pros if and when I decide to install

a permanent perimeter fence. The pros figure to be less expensive once all my time and aggravation are factored in, and I'm convinced the final product will look much better.

Above: Hazen the guard llama scans a flock of Shetland ewes at Maple Ridge Sheep Farm. Guard animals, fencing, and electricity are effective methods for keeping predators away.

If your overall goal is to raise a few sheep without hiring pros or sinking a bunch of money into the effort, however, here's the simplest and cheapest way to go: buy a half dozen lambs in the spring, buy the lambs one of those metal and canvas carport roofs that are all the rage these days, throw in an inexpensive electric-fence charger and a few rolls of portable electric netting for fencing, and you're practically home. After the lambs "matriculate" in the fall, you can easily dismantle the whole operation and store it in your garage until next year.

In any event, check the Web sites of the national equipment suppliers (see the tools and equipment appendix) for more complete instructions on the installation and costs of various fencing options. The Premier 1 fencing catalog, in particular, is a very helpful and comprehensive fencing resource.

CHAPTER SIX

Rams and Breeding

Although rams are equal partners in the creation of new lambs, they seem to present more than their share of management headaches for the small-time shepherd. Basically, you want one to show up at your place for about forty-five days each fall, vigorous and strong and ready to go, and then disappear back where he came from the other ten and a half months of the year. But that's a difficult logistical feat to pull off.

You want your ewes to give birth to their lambs during a nice, warm, spring week that is convenient for you. A ram, meanwhile, wants to impregnate the ewes every chance he gets; leave him alone with your flock for a year, and you'll have lambs being born all across the calendar. Your only option to prevent nature from taking its course is to keep the ram separate from the ewes for all except the fall breeding season.

But this is problematic too. Sheep are social animals—you can't just tie your ram to a tree out in the back forty for ten months. He will, quite literally, go crazy. Even two sheep together seem to suffer from isolation, and the consensus among small-time shepherds is that three sheep is the minimum number required for healthy ovine socialization. You can see the problem unfolding: what started as a need for six weeks of ram-hood in November has suddenly turned into you owning an entire second flock, complete with its own shelter, fencing, feeders, hay supply, and so on.

Here are several ways to approach the ram challenge, each with its advantages and disadvantages.

Opposite: Mikey, a Romney ram lamb, takes in a visitor to the Mathewson home. He was later sold to another farm to be used for breeding.

RENT-A-RAM

The simplest option is to call up your trusted neighbor and work out a deal to borrow a ram for six weeks, usually in exchange for a stud fee of $30 to $50 (or often $10 per ewe) or the pick of the lamb crop. Particularly if you don't need a purebred ram to maintain your purebred breed, you should have lots of options out there, even if you don't live in the heart of sheep country. No solution is simpler than this. When you need the ram, he's there; when you don't, he's not your problem. There's no danger of a ram jumping a fence and impregnating your ewes prematurely—you have no ram on the premises.

The downside is that swapping animals between farms potentially allows worms, bacteria, and diseases to make the trip as well. For this reason, many shepherds are reluctant to swap animals around. Foot rot, in particular, is both highly contagious and notoriously difficult to eradicate. You may think twice about bringing an animal from a larger sheep farm (with its inherent susceptibility to disease and infection) to your smaller operation.

In addition, if your neighbor has a prized stud ram on the premises, he or she is likely to be using him for breeding at just the time you'd like to bring him to your place. You may have to move your own breeding time earlier or later in the year, which entails either lambs being born in cold weather or lambs being still quite small come fall slaughter. However, if you can find a neighbor you know and trust who is willing to work with you on the vagaries of schedule and sanitation, no option is simpler and neater than the rent-a-ram approach.

BUY A STUD FOR SLAUGHTER

Your next simplest option is to buy a stud ram, use him for six weeks, and then slaughter him for meat. This could be a mature "proven" ram, which means he's successfully sired lambs in the past; in this case, you'll end up with a good supply of mutton afterwards. Or you could get a six-month-old ram lamb who is not yet proven but whose meat can still be sold as lamb afterwards. You can even time it right so that the stud ram goes to slaughter along with the lambs you've been raising all summer.

The advantages here are the relative simplicity of the deal (like the rent-a-ram approach, you'll only have a ram at your place for six weeks or so). You'll have additional meat to eat or sell afterwards. And since you won't be sending the stud

Above: Bode, a two-year-old Romney ram, started breeding ewes at six months old at the Mathewson home. Bode is put in with the ewes in November so lambing will occur in April.

ram back to his home farm, other shepherds will jump at the chance to sell you a stud since there's no potential reintroduction sanitation problem for them to worry about.

There is still the sanitation problem for you to contend with, however. You want to make sure that any stud ram you buy is clean and healthy himself and comes from a clean and healthy flock. If you buy a ram lamb, there's the question of his potency, since he's never had the chance to prove himself before. A ram lamb should be fully potent by six months of age, but "should" implies an element of doubt; if the ram is on the small side, or not in top form, or just not potent, you won't know for sure until spring, at

 Above: Romney ram lambs tussle at Landgoes Farm. Avoid becoming too friendly with a ram lamb if you're planning to use him for breeding later on.

which point you'll be going an entire year without any lambs. But if you buy an older, proven ram, there's the question of what to do with the mutton; the market for mutton is far less bustling than the market for lamb (see the meat and slaughter chapter for more on mutton). Either way, you're trading the convenience of not owning your own ram flock for the risk of not being quite sure what you're getting.

OWN YOUR OWN RAM

The final option is to own your own ram. This gives you the most control but also requires the most work and expense. I have yet to do this, but after trying the previous two options several times, I'm thinking more and more about it. The breakthrough for me has been the knowledge that, while a ram needs company, it doesn't have to be the company of other rams.

I once worked on a farm that had a flock of a dozen breeding ewes and a second "herd" consisting of the stud ram and two beef cows. The ram and the beefers had a fine time together most of the year out on the back pastures away from the ewes and lambs. When his services were required, the ram was brought in out of the cold for six weeks of glory and then returned to exile with the beefers. The farmers neatly solved the ram problem while simultaneously having some tasty beef to add to the chest freezer every now and again.

The downside of this approach is self-evident: a second flock requires completely separate facilities, plus their own supply of hay for the winter. If the ram and ewes are going to be housed in close proximity, the fencing and gates need to be top notch if they're to keep randy ram from jumping the gun. If this isn't something you can or want to pull off, then go back to either the rent-a-ram or slaughter-a-ram options. But if you already live on an old farm with a bunch of outbuildings crying out for use, this may be the approach for you.

Your ram's companions don't need to be beef cows. They could be horses or llamas or goats or other rams, depending on what you want or need. Keep in mind that, if it's horses, you need to make sure that the fencing is built for the ram (woven wire or high-tensile electric) and not the horses (that flimsy white tape that horses somehow mistake for a fence). Your ram will happily walk under the horse tape and saunter over to the ewe flock at the first sniff of estrus.

Another consideration when owning your own ram is that, sooner or later, you're going to want to breed him to a ewe that was originally his lamb. Unless you're an expert geneticist trying to capture a unique trait or create a new breed of sheep, you'll want to avoid such experimental inbreeding. That means you'll either need a new ram every few years or else you'll have to buy your replacement ewes from some other farm. So owning your own ram flock doesn't completely insulate you from the outside world: you'll still have to buy in either a fresh ram or fresh ewes every few years.

A couple I know keeps a ram flock consisting of a wether ram (a castrated male who serves as the elder statesman of the flock), a stud ram, and a ram lamb who is being groomed to be the future stud ram. This allows the shepherds to both keep their favorite ram lamb each year and give him another year to grow before being pressed into service. Obviously the relationship between ewes and rams can become somewhat complicated, since you don't want to breed a ram lamb back to his mother. But if you're up for the full-bore shepherding experience, this is the way to go.

LIVING WITH RAMS

Although much of this chapter so far has portrayed rams as nothing but a hassle for the small-time shepherd, I should say that rams and ram lambs are a lot of fun to be around. They are much more gregarious and social than ewes and are quicker to come over and say hello to new faces in the barnyard. They have a certain confidence and swagger that comes, especially if they have horns, from being the ovine version of "armed and dangerous."

Actually, armed and dangerous in the human sense, too. If you're working in a pen with a full-grown ram, you'd do well never to turn your back on him. The ram will certainly attempt, at some point, to take you down a peg with a hard butt to your butt or, worse yet, someplace less padded. These events are usually more injurious to the shepherd's pride than body, but you don't want to stake your health and happiness on "usually."

Harder still, if you're raising a ram lamb that you know is going to be used for breeding purposes later in life, is avoiding the temptation to cuddle and scratch him when he's a youngster. If he grows up thinking that humans are not to be feared, he will likely become unmanageably dangerous once he reaches full size. Rams live in an hierarchical world, and if you (or someone else) teaches them that humans are low-ranking softies, they will never miss a chance to try to assert their dominance.

Finally, rams, thanks to their hard skulls, can and will kill one another if given the chance. For moral and financial reasons, your job as shepherd is to prevent this from happening. Whenever you are putting two or more

rams together in a single pen or pasture, you must first hold them in your confinement pen or shelter for twelve to twenty-four hours to allow them to get acquainted (or reacquainted) without sufficient running room to cause each other injury. Give them room to sniff each other, jostle, and take a step or two to butt heads—but no more.

 Above: A group of Shetland yearling rams walks down a laneway at Maple Ridge Sheep Farm. Farmer Linda Doane said her rams are more docile when kept together.

After they've established their hierarchy in the relative safety of this smaller area, you can let them loose in the barnyard or pasture without worry of major damage.

RAM CONFORMATION

Regardless of whether you rent, borrow, buy, raise, or steal your stud ram, you should have a rough idea of what to look for in a good breeding ram. There are the usual signs: he looks nice, has good wool, is muscular, scores between 3 and 4 at breeding time (to insure he'll have stamina), has nice intact hooves, and generally seems the picture of health. Then there are two other factors to consider: testicle size and growth rate.

Without going to the bother and expense (and, I would imagine, embarrassment) of having your ram's semen tested for potency, you can get a sense of whether or not your proposed stud ram is going to have what it takes by assessing the size of his testicular sack. If it's large, your man likely has the goods. If not, he may be short on testosterone and potency. Large is, of course, a relative thing that varies between breeds, and I wouldn't be too hung up on getting the biggest boy in the bunch. But if you go to a farm to buy a potential stud ram, or if you're trying to decide among your crop of current ram lambs, make sure your guy isn't the runt of the litter in this most-important department. In the final analysis, it's not his personality that you're interested in.

The second ram attribute to consider is how quickly he grew as a lamb. Whereas the ability to throw twins or triplets is an attribute passed on primarily by the ewe, growth and vigor are passed on primarily through the ram. A ram lamb that grew quickly and vigorously will likely pass that trait on to his offspring, whereas a ram lamb that is still small at six months of age will likely produce similarly slow-growing lambs. This can lead to a terrible decision come autumn, when your favorite, cute little ram lamb needs to be sent to slaughter. But once again, cute isn't the key attribute you're looking for in a stud ram.

BREEDING SCHEDULE

Ewes come into heat for approximately thirty hours every seventeen days. If all went according to an ideal schedule, therefore, you could put a ram in with your ewes for eighteen days and be sure he'd impregnated all of them. In the actual case, however, there are uncertainties.

It's possible that a ewe lamb came into heat at just the time that the ram was busy servicing an older ewe with a stronger appeal, so he missed the youngster. It's also possible that some of the ewes hadn't started their fall estrus by the time the ram arrived and hence weren't fertile right away. (In the wild, most ungulates will only conceive in the autumn. Domesticated sheep, by and large, have had this natural limitation bred out of them, but some breeds still retain their fall-only predilection.)

There are two ways to improve the odds of a 100% conception rate. First, put the ram in with the ewes suddenly—don't keep him penned up next door for a few weeks beforehand. The sudden arrival of testosterone on the scene can trigger any autumn-only ewes to begin their estrus cycle upon his arrival. Second, keep the ram in with the ewes longer than the eighteen-day theoretical minimum. Five to six weeks is ideal, since it should give the ram two opportunities with each ewe and will mean that the ram is with the ewes later into the fall to catch those autumn-only stragglers.

Both the ram and the ewes need to be in top physical shape in order for conception to be successful, so make sure each animal is scoring a 3 to 3+ during the breeding season. If the ram is underweight, he may lack the potency or the stamina to service all the ewes. (One ram for every thirty or so ewes is considered an acceptable ratio, assuming the ram is in decent shape.) The ewes need to be both in good shape and on a rising plane of nutrition for maximum conception to take place, because the chances of them conceiving triplets, twins, singles, or no lambs at all is based partly on their nutritional shape come breeding time. In the chapter on feeding, we went into more detail on flushing the ewes prior to breeding time, but the summary is that ewes should be fed supplemental grain for three weeks before and three weeks after the ram's visit, plus during the visit itself.

Above: Spice was one of the original Navajo-Churro rams at The Land & Lamb Co. He died of old age in 2002.

RAM LAMB CONSIDERATIONS

Ram lambs potentially reach sexual potency starting at about four months of age. If you are looking to rent or buy a ram lamb for breeding, therefore, an animal that is six months of age should be good to go. The flip side is, if you have ram lambs in your summer flock, they need to be separated from the ewes after their first four months of life. Once again, this may mean having separate facilities for them for their last few months before being sold or slaughtered. Or, if you'd rather not go this route, be sure to castrate your ram lambs in the spring so that they can stay with the main flock right through the fall.

EWE LAMB CONSIDERATIONS

Whereas ram lambs reach sexual potency starting at about four months of age, ewe lambs usually don't mature until six months or so. This brings up the question of whether or not to breed them their first fall. If you are doing everything possible to avoid running two flocks, just leave your ewe lambs in with the ewes and let nature take its course. You're more than likely to find, come springtime, that they are carrying lambs.

Some shepherds, however, prefer to prevent their ewe lambs from being bred that first year. The main advantage of waiting a year is that a ewe lamb will be able to put more energy into growing that first winter, which will potentially make her larger and stronger for the rest of her life. She will also have the opportunity to watch the older ewes go through a lambing season, so she won't be so surprised and confused when her turn comes the following year. And finally, since many ewe lambs only conceive a single lamb that first season, the economic downside of not lambing in year one may be more than recouped by a larger ewe who throws good-sized twins every year thereafter.

ADVANCED TWO-FLOCK BREEDING MANAGEMENT

If you're an expert at that childhood riddle in which a farmer has to cross a river carrying a fox, a chicken, and a bag of grain, but can only take one item at a time in the canoe and wants to make the crossing without losing either the chicken or the grain, you're probably starting to see some management possibilities here for a two-flock system. It goes like this. In the spring and early summer, the ewes and all the lambs are in one flock, the ram and the beefers are in the other. At midsummer, move all the lambs in with the ram and beefers during weaning. Later in the summer, move the ewe lambs back in with the ewes. At breeding time, send all the ram lambs and any to-be-eaten ewe lambs to slaughter, and swap the ram with the keeper ewe lambs so that the ewe lambs are in with the beefers and the ram is with the ewes. When breeding is over, swap the ewe lambs with the ram so that the ewes are all together and the ram is back with the beefers. Repeat next year. Simple as that.

In case you never heard the riddle about the farmer, she takes the chicken over on the first load, goes back across empty; takes the grain across on the second load and comes back with the chicken; takes the fox across on the third load and comes back empty; and finishes by taking the chicken across (again) as the final load.

CHAPTER SEVEN

Raising Your Own Lambs

Without a doubt, lambing is the most exciting, rewarding, complicated, and nerve-racking season in the shepherd's year. Life and death are on the line.

Despite the horror stories you have heard about lambing (why is it that if you mention the idea of raising sheep to someone, they invariably tell you tales of woe about everything that can possibly go wrong?), most lambing happens so easily that you don't even need to be there. Ewes have been giving birth to lambs since time immemorial, and while our breeding efforts for meat and wool have not made it go any easier, lambing is nevertheless an instinctive event that usually goes smoothly. Rest assured that your ewes know far more about lambing than you will ever need to.

My approach to lambing is more like that of a proud parent and midwife than that of a heavily armed physician. If I can reduce the stress on the ewe and her lambs while delighting in the birth of the new animals, so much the better. Nature is going to do its thing; I simply try to reduce the discomfort and shorten the moments of uncertainty. A ewe is going to lick her lambs dry, for example, so I simply try to help out with a towel to speed things up. The lamb is going to try to suckle its mother's teats, so I nudge the lamb in the right direction. That sort of thing.

This isn't to say that disaster doesn't loom during lambing. It does. But provided you've been managing your ewes well and feeding them appropriately (not too much and not too little), the probability of disaster is low.

Opposite: Crepe, a Navajo-Churro ewe lamb Marian White brought home from New Mexico, lifts its head to see a visitor to the farm.

You'll be able to deal with the most common problems yourself. And assuming you've already established a relationship with a local vet, you'll have the backup of a medical professional in the event you lose your nerve or come up against an especially difficult situation.

IS SHE PREGNANT?

Winter visitors to our farm often ask, "Are the sheep pregnant?" To which I must honestly reply, "I have no idea!" Unlike human pregnancy, which unfolds in a more-or-less linear fashion with the mother looking progressively larger and larger, ewes will show almost no evidence of being pregnant until the final six weeks or so. Add a thick, wooly fleece into the mix, and it can be difficult to tell who is pregnant and who isn't—even with only a few weeks to go.

Shepherds whose livelihood depends on their sheep being pregnant can use ultrasound and other tools to sense who is pregnant and who needs more time with the ram. For small-timers like me, it's just wait and see. If a proven ram had forty-five days with the ewes, the chances are extremely high that all of the ewes are pregnant. The main telltale sign I watch for is enlargement of the udder, which starts to happen in the final few weeks. Or better yet, I ask our shearer when he comes to shear, which is usually about three weeks before the first possible lambing date. He's handled so many sheep in his life that he can tell as soon as he sits a ewe on her butt for shearing whether or not she's pregnant.

Of course, knowing the first possible lambing date helps you know when to start looking for signs. Ewes gestate for an average of 148 days. Figure out the date your ram first had access to your ewes, count forward 148 days, and mark your calendar. Now go back three days and mark this date as your earliest possible lamb date. (Sheep gestation is much more predictable than human gestation, but even so, a ewe could deliver a day or two prior to full term.) For quick reference, there is a Ewe Gestation Table in the back of this book (see page 222).

THE TYPICAL BIRTH

As with all aspects of shepherding, your first goal in lambing is to get a feel for what "normal" is. Once you have a lambing season or two under your belt, you'll be far quicker to relax and enjoy it—because you'll realize that major problems are rare. Plus, you'll have the confidence of knowing a potential problem when you see one.

In the meantime, here is my best account of what a typical birth is like. Several days before giving birth, your ewe will start acting oddly now and then. She'll stare off into space, often with her head lowered, and may even face into a corner of the barn away from the flock. She may paw the ground as if preparing a nest. She's liable to be standing up while the others are lying down, or vice versa. She'll spend time looking over her shoulder, watching her back. In general, she won't seem like her usual self. Her udder will rapidly start to fill out, and her vulva may swell.

Usually within a few hours of giving birth, the lambs will "drop" into their birthing position inside the ewe. Instead of resting up near the ewe's spine, almost like bicycle saddlebags, they will shift down into her gut, and the area along the ewe's lumbar spine will start to look hollowed out. This is a difficult transition to describe, but once you've seen it a few times, you'll know what you're looking at. It isn't crucial that you recognize this in advance, but it's simply helpful for planning.

When birth is imminent, the ewe will go into obvious contractions, often grinding her teeth against her upper palate with each contraction. She will typically paw at the ground between contractions and will tend to lie down with each contraction and stand up between them. She may also start to nicker, which is a very distinctive gurgling in the back of her throat that she'll use to gather and comfort her lambs once they are born. She's just getting the about-to-be-born lambs used to her voice.

As the contractions grow stronger and birth begins, you will see a tiny nose and pair of front hooves emerge from the ewe's vagina. Alternatively, you may see the amniotic sac emerge first, part of which may hang outside the ewe and fill partially with fluid. A few more pushes, and the lamb will slide right out of the ewe, safely tucked inside the protective cushion of the

 Above: Linda Doane pets Razzledazzle, a Shetland ewe lamb, at Maple Ridge Sheep Farm.

amniotic sack, and land on the ground. If there are twins or triplets, a half-hour might pass between births. Usually, however, all lambs are born within five or ten minutes of the first one. I assume that there are multiple lambs in there, just to be safe. But it's impossible to tell in advance.

The ewe will quickly break the amniotic sack around the lamb (if it hasn't broken already) and concentrate on clearing the lamb's nose and mouth so that it can breathe on its own. From there, she will work over the next hour

or so to completely clean and dry the lambs by licking them all over.

Once they start breathing, the lambs will work almost at once at trying to stand up. Within a half-hour to an hour, often with the help of aggressive nudging and licking from momma, they will usually succeed. The ewe will try to corral the lambs back toward her udder, and once there, she will lick under the lambs' tails to both stimulate suckling and remove the amniotic poop from the lamb, called *myconium*. After a few false starts, the lamb will manage to drink a little bit from a teat and then, with little fanfare, will lie down and fall quickly asleep. Sometimes, the lambs will grab a quick nap after standing for the first time and before they attempt to tackle the udder.

The ewe, meanwhile, will take some good slurps of water and eat a little hay. There is likely to be a long strip or two of placenta hanging out of her vulva, which will fall out within one to four hours as the ewe expels the placenta. She will let her lambs nap for a bit before rousing them and encouraging them to drink more from her udder, usually working on one lamb at a time in succession. After a few rounds of this, the lambs will be strong enough (and hungry enough) to wake up on their own and find momma. At which point, both lambs and ewe are pretty much in the clear.

Your Role During Lambing

What is your role in all this? Be helpful but not overly aggressive. As the lambs are born, help to clear their noses and dry them off. You'll want to let the ewe take the lead on this, since this process helps cement the bond between the ewe and lamb; but feel free to work on one lamb while the ewe is concentrating on another (in the event that there are twins).

Your next task is to move the ewe and lambs into a corner of the pen and fence them off from the rest of the flock. This will give the new family a chance to get acquainted with less risk of becoming separated or trampled. Move the lambs into the pen slowly so the ewe can see you doing it: she will gladly follow them. If you take the lambs away at this point or cause her to lose sight of them, she will be unduly stressed and may even reject the lambs later under the misconception that they aren't hers. The best approach is to slowly carry the lambs at ground level over to their pen, with the ewe licking them and nickering as she goes. Do this as soon as you reasonably can. The best time is once all the lambs are born but before they can stand up on their own.

Once everyone is penned in together, use a pair of sharp scissors to trim each lamb's umbilical cord, leaving an inch or so still attached to the lamb. (The cord itself will have broken during birth, so the lamb won't still be attached to the placenta at this point.) The one-inch stub that you leave on the lamb will shrivel and fall off on its own in a week or so. Dip this protruding bit of cord into iodine to sterilize the opening and reduce the risk of infection.

Next, squirt a shot of lamb-saver gel into the mouth of each lamb. This is sort of an insurance policy for the youngster—a charge of nutrition and minerals to help give him or her enough strength to find momma and make the transition to suckling. Make sure the gel is at room temperature (70°F or so) so it won't congeal in the lamb's mouth. Giving this gel is obviously an extra step—one that would not occur in the wild, but a step that seems to give the little critters a boost while giving the shepherd the pleasure of having been helpful in some way.

Finally, make sure the ewe has access to hay and water as she will be quite hungry and thirsty once she's finished cleaning up her lambs. Add

about a cup of molasses per gallon of water, and make the water warm so that the ewe is sure to drink it. Don't give her grain just yet because it is quite rich and could cause her to produce

Above: A purebred Southdown lamb rests in the straw bedding at Fat Rooster Farm.

more milk than the newborn lambs can drink. Good quality hay is perfect. You'll want to arrange the food and water in such a way that the lambs can't stumble into it and become trapped. Use a high-sided water bucket, and drizzle in a few gobs of molasses as a special treat for the proud mother.

That's it! Now you just sit back and delight in the magic that's taking place at your farm.

PREPARING FOR LAMBING

Now that you have a sense of what a typical birth is like, there are a few things you'll want to do in advance to get ready. Your stress level and the stress level of your ewes and lambs will be greatly reduced if you've made adequate preparations and have the equipment you need, placed where you'll need it. The steps outlined below tell you what you need to know.

1. **Determine your first possible lamb date,** as discussed above.

2. **Meet your vet.** If you haven't done this already, make a connection with your local vet either by visiting his or her office or—better yet—by arranging a visit to your farm. I have never had to call our vet during lambing time, but that's hardly the point: knowing that the vet is available allows me to sleep soundly at night.

3. **Clean the pen.** You and a bunch of newly born little lambs are about to spend lots of time in close proximity to the floor of your barn or shelter. If this floor is emitting wafts of ammonia from a winter's worth of soiled bedding, this is going to be less than pleasant for all concerned. Whenever possible, clean out your shelter in advance of lambing season and put down fresh bedding. "Unsanitary" is obviously a relative term, given that sheep walk around in and sleep in poop all the time. But unsanitary conditions, meaning wet bedding, ammonia, and slimy bedding or flooring, can make your newborn lambs sick.

4. **Set up the jugs.** The small pen that you put each ewe into with her lamb(s) is called the *lambing jug*. This pen should ideally be two to three times larger than the ewe herself: large enough for her to turn around, but not so large that lambs are likely to get far away from her. Four feet by four feet or four feet by six feet are tried-and-true sizes. Make sure it isn't too drafty in the jug, and if the weather is cold (say, below 40°F), arrange for a light bulb or heat lamp to help the lambs warm during their first twenty-four hours. Go ahead and set up the jugs before lambing season begins so that, during the exciting minutes after birth, you simply have to move the ewe and lambs in and close the door;

you're not going to want to be rummaging around in the barn for scrap lumber and spare nails at this point.

You'll want a minimum of two jugs in the event that two of your ewes give birth at once, and figure on roughly one jug for every eight or ten ewes thereafter. Work out the details of how you are going to get food and water into each jug, and set this up in advance too. Make sure that any troughs or buckets are deep enough or far enough off the ground so the lambs won't be able to climb in and get stuck.

Don't put a laboring ewe into the jug before she delivers. She'll want space to walk around and paw out a nest during delivery and will be less stressed if you let her do that. Just have the jug ready to go at a moment's notice.

5. **Arrange your tools.** Though you won't need much equipment for a normal lambing, you'll want it all in a clean, convenient place. Here are the items you'll need (consult the appendix on tools and equipment for more details):

   a. Clean towels
   b. Sharp scissors
   c. Iodine, in a small container (like a film canister)
   d. Lamb-saver gel
   e. Disposable gloves
   f. Molasses
   g. Pencil and paper, to record dates, times, potential names, and weight
   h. Scale for weighing the lambs

   In addition, here are some items to have on hand that you will only need in the event that the birth is somewhat complicated:

   a. J-Jelly
   b. Elbow-length disposable gloves
   c. Rubber snare or string
   d. Lamb-saver kit: syringe and tube
   e. Colostrum, powdered or frozen
   f. Powdered milk replacer
   g. Baby bottle with nipples

6. **Close the gate.** When you sense that a birth is imminent, it's helpful to confine all your ewes together in their shelter so that lambs aren't born out in a pasture somewhere. Confining just the ewe in question would cause her great distress at being separated from her flock in her hour of need, so confine everyone together. The others may complain a bit, but can usually be placated with a few flakes of hay. If you are going to be away from the farm during lambing time, close the animals in then, too, to make sure that any lambs born during your absence have the advantage of being indoors.

7. **Stay home.** Lambing season is not the time to schedule vacations to the tropics or even weekends away with friends. You'll start to get a sense of when a birth is not imminent, which will enable you to slip away here and there to attend to the other details in your life. If you have an off-the-farm job nearby, arrange to come home at noon to see how everyone is doing. But in general, do what you can to be home as much as possible. Your ewes will appreciate knowing you're around, and you'll feel much better too. You're going to be thinking about lambing anyway—so why not do it at home, where you can satisfy your curiosity with a peek in the barn, rather than far away where you can only wonder and worry?

YOUR ROLE IN LAMBING: THREE PHASES

Your role in lambing can be roughly divided into three phases: getting the lambs on the ground, getting the lambs established, and sending the lambs on their way. Here's a look at each of these phases, along with some of the most common difficulties that may come your way during each phase.

PHASE ONE: GETTING THE LAMBS ON THE GROUND

This first phase is relatively straightforward: if the ewe is inside in a clean, draft-free shelter with an open jug nearby at the time of birth, you're off to a great start. Active labor may last one to three hours, so resist the temptation to jump into the pen with a ewe at the first sign of action. A first-time mother,

in particular, may require several hours to work through a perfectly normal delivery.

When does a delivery stop being normal? This is the key question, and it's a judgment call that will become easier for you to make over time. The most likely problem you'll encounter during birthing is that the lamb is too large to easily slide out through the birth canal.

Above: Knox climbs over her mother, Bragg, while Dix tries to nurse in the barnyard at The Land & Lamb Co. Owner Marian White said the ewe lambs were sold to an 11-year-old who would be entering the Navajo-Churros in 4-H competitions.

(Make a note to feed your ewes less next winter!) Often, the forehead and forefeet will emerge, but after another thirty minutes or so of hard labor, and despite the exertions of the ewe, the lamb will seem stuck. At the thirty-minute mark, put on a pair of disposable gloves (to help keep things sterile) and smear some J-Jelly on the vulva where the lamb's head emerges. You can often slide a finger an inch or so inside to help spread the lubricant and work the flesh back from around the lamb's forehead. This may help the lamb slide out.

 Above: Guthrie, a purebred Shetland ram lamb, makes his voice heard at Maple Ridge Sheep Farm.

If it doesn't, then the problem lies not with the soft tissue but with the lamb's shoulders being stuck against the pelvis. Grab hold of the head and forefeet of the lamb and pull gently out and down, away from the ewe's tail and toward her lower legs. This will help extend the lamb's neck and pull it through the pelvis.

If this doesn't work after a few tries, you need to cock the lamb's shoulders so that one shoulder comes through the pelvis ahead of the other. Pull one of the lamb's legs forward as far as it will easily go while pushing the other leg back until it is almost fully back inside the ewe. This action will effectively reduce the lamb's cross-section and help ease it through the pelvis.

You want to be gentle during all this, yet firm and forceful. Provided you pull the lamb directly out of the ewe, without twisting or jerking it, there is very little harm you can cause. Plus, you can do a lot of good by minimizing the time that lamb and ewe spend in this uncomfortable position. But if cocking the lamb's shoulders still has not freed it, call the vet right away. The quicker a vet can come and assist you, the better.

The second problem you may encounter is that the lamb presents itself in some configuration other than head plus forelegs; head plus one foreleg is most common, though rear legs only or front legs without head are also possible. Wash your hands and arm and/or put on a disposable shoulder-length glove if you have one. Your goal is to reach inside the ewe and arrange the lamb so that it presents itself with its head together with its forelegs. In any other configuration, the lamb may not fit through the birth canal.

Depending on your confidence, budget, and location, you may want to call the vet to do this, at least the first time. There could be up to three heads and a dozen legs inside the ewe's womb, and you can't shine a flashlight inside her to see what is going on. Everything is done by feel.

The one abnormal position that you should tackle yourself is the two rear legs presentation. Just grab the rear legs and pull out and down. Do this as soon as you are sure it's rear legs you are dealing with—the umbilical chord may be crushed prematurely during a backwards birth, so time is of the essence to get the lamb outside and into breathable air

One helpful trick for other presentations is to use lengths of string or a specially designed rubber snare to keep track of the forelegs and head as you identify them. Pull a foreleg out of the ewe, attach the string, and push the leg back inside. Once you find the matching front leg by following the string and first foreleg up across the shoulders, attach a string to the second leg and loop one around the head. Now take hold of all three strings and line all three up in normal delivery position—which is hooves underneath the head, with the head on the tail side of the vagina and the hooves on the leg side. Make sure no umbilical cords or other lambs are in the way and gently work the lamb out through the birth canal, letting the ewe do the pushing if she's able.

Daunted? Well, you should be: this is not for the faint of heart. Remember, you can call the vet at any time. And remember too that the vast majority of births happen so easily that everything is fine—even if you aren't there keeping an eye on things.

During our second year of lambing, our eldest ewe had difficulty with a stuck lamb. (It turned out she gave birth to a twelve-pound and an eight-pound lamb: eight pounds is considered average, twelve is enormous!) A friend of mine stood outside the pen, flipping through a book, reading me the instructions about how to free the shoulders of a stuck lamb. Although I was too intent on the problem to see the comedy of the situation at the time, we laugh about it now. He would read me a few sentences, and I'd yell back, "OK, what next?" Occasionally, when the text seemed inadequate for the situation at hand, I'd yell back, "That's it? Isn't there anything else written on that page??"

The ewe eventually delivered both lambs just beautifully. The eight-pounder, in fact, slipped out about a minute after the first one while I wasn't looking. Neither ewe nor lambs were worse for wear at the end of it all and, I confess, I felt the distinct puffiness of pride for having held up under pressure and assisted at the key moment.

Of course, there are a whole universe of potential birthing problems whose likelihood of occurrence is very small, but the prospect can end up looming very large in the mind of the novice shepherd. My advice is: don't let them. Just call the vet. The cases I've described above are both the most likely and the most fixable problems. Later, if you discover that ovine obstetrics is your life's calling, you can buy additional books that describe lambing problems in all their glory.

PHASE TWO: GETTING THE LAMBS ESTABLISHED

Once the lambs are on the ground, your overall goal is to get them dry and nursing from a fed and happy momma. Job one is to make sure the lambs are breathing by helping to clear their noses and encouraging the ewe to lick them. Jostling the lamb around a bit also seems to remind it that it's been born and should begin to breathe. Tickling the lamb's nostrils with a piece of straw will cause it to sneeze and is another way to encourage breathing.

If, for some reason, neither cleaning, jostling, nor tickling the lamb does the trick, I've read that you should grab the lamb by its hind legs and spin it in an arc from over your head to down by your feet; the centrifugal force is said to clear the amniotic fluid from the lamb's airway and stimulate the

Right: A Katahdin lamb and mother watch a visitor to the pasture before the start of a sheep dog trial at Steve Wetmore's farm.

lungs to start breathing. I suppose I would do this if, indeed, the lamb wasn't breathing; but the logistics of holding onto a slippery lamb while spinning it around without smashing it into the ground or hay loft seem anything but straightforward. So far, every one of my lambs has begun breathing on its own within a minute or two of being born.

As soon as the lambs are breathing, move the lambs and ewe into their own lambing jug, separate from the flock, where ewe and lambs can cement their bond and the ewe can relax without worrying about the whereabouts of her lambs. How long should the animals remain together in the jug? One to three days is typical. One day might be for a veteran ewe who clearly has the job in hand and is informing you of her desire to rejoin the flock. Three days might be for a novice ewe (especially one that has lambed early in the season without having watched the other ewes) who still seems unclear on the details of nursing. I've observed that my first-time ewes learn the ropes from their more experienced flock-mates, but I nevertheless keep an extra eye out for them and give them as much time in the jug as they need.

When one ewe is in a jug and the rest of the flock is not, your overall management strategy becomes somewhat complicated. The one ewe isn't going to like being left behind if the rest of the flock heads off to graze on a distant pasture. But the flock may become restless when penned up for days on end—and the still-pregnant ewes could benefit from exercise in the last days of gestation. I usually work out some sort of compromise between the pen and the pasture—depending on the ewe, the weather, and my schedule. There's no right answer here, but just something to be aware of.

With the ewe and lambs now safely in their jug, this is the best time to trim the umbilical cord if it's longer than one inch or so. You'll also need to dip the end in iodine to disinfect it. The best item to use for this is a good, old-fashioned film canister: fill the canister two-thirds full of iodine, press the canister up against the lamb's belly, and gently flip the lamb over briefly to soak the whole cord. Press the canister tightly to the belly to prevent spillage, and wear gloves, if possible; this will keep your fingers from resembling those of a chain smoker.

If you want to weigh the newborns, now is also a good time. The ideal weighing arrangement is a sling that hangs from a spring scale so the lamb can flail its legs without tipping the scale over. Whatever you do, be careful to minimize the amount of time that the lamb is separated from the ewe during this crucial bonding period. A few minutes is fine, but a half-hour of petting and cooing is much too long at this early stage.

The next step is to make sure the lamb gets its first suckle from momma's teat. If you are so inclined, "strip" the ewe's teats first to establish the flow of milk. To milk a sheep, make an "OK" sign with your thumb and index finger, slide this circle up to the top of the teat (palm facing the floor), pinch your thumb and index finger tightly around the top of the teat, and then slide your middle finger down the teat, squeezing out milk as you go. When you reach the bottom, release your thumb and index finger to allow the teat to refill, and repeat.

It may take a few minutes for the teats to fill initially with milk. Massage the udder if needed, which will stimulate the ewe to "let down" her milk. Once you get a good squirt of somewhat clear, white-colored milk out of each teat, you're all set. Leave the rest for the lamb. Help the lambs locate the teats by nudging them in the right direction. The ewe will help with this too; in all likelihood, the ewe and lamb will figure all of this out without any assistance at all.

This first milk from the ewe is called *colostrum*, and it is rich in the nutrients and antibodies needed by the lambs. A lamb is born with an immune system that is only partially developed and lacks antibodies of its own. It is therefore crucial that the lamb drink colostrum in its first few hours of life to receive antibodies from its mother and fully develop its own immune system.

I confess that I find keeping track of whether or not a lamb is nursing to be the most maddening part of lambing. Baby lambs don't drink much milk, and sometimes it seems as if they bounce off the teat without ever really attaching. Plus, a newborn lamb spends almost its entire first day sleeping, which I have tended to misinterpret as dying if I'm convinced they haven't suckled effectively.

 Above: A Southdown ewe lamb looks out the window of the barn at Fat Rooster Farm. Farmers Jennifer Megyesi and Kyle Jones breed animals for organic meat.

The ewe, still unfamiliar with the feeling of a suckling lamb, may also step away from a lamb after only a few seconds of suckling. But a few seconds is all it takes. Before I started raising lambs, I imagined that they drank their mother's milk for minutes at a time—like a milking machine in a dairy parlor or a human baby. But that is never true with lambs. Even two-month-olds will rarely suckle for more than five seconds at a time. Their strategy is the old hit and run.

Rather than try to crane my neck and observe every possible suckling, which is impossible, I instead make the assumption that everything is going fine. I assume that the lambs are sneaking colostrum, even if I don't see it happening. Then I keep a weather eye out for one of the two key signs that suggests that a lamb isn't suckling: its mouth is cold, or it doesn't stretch when it stands up.

The key indicator of a lamb that isn't suckling is a cold mouth. Gently work the end of your pinky finger into the corner of the lamb's mouth. It should be warm in there, and the lamb should either attempt to suckle your finger or try to spit it out. How warm is warm? Stick your pinkie in your own mouth (you might want to do this before you stick it in the lamb's mouth): that's the kind of warm you're looking for. If the lamb's mouth is warm, it's getting enough milk, regardless of whether or not you've seen it happen.

The second indicator of a healthy lamb is that it will stretch its spine every time it stands up. If it fails to stretch, it may also have a hunched back—a sure sign that it is cold and stiff. You'll notice that all of your lambs are slightly hunched during their first few hours of life and that their spines straighten out once they warm up and start suckling. A lamb that doesn't stretch, or whose back stays rounded and hunched while standing, or whose mouth is cold, is in need of further assistance.

In the immediate term, you need to warm the little guy (or gal) up. Fully drying the lamb with towels may be enough, as will placing it under a light bulb or heat lamp to give it some external energy. Plan B is to bring the lamb inside your house and pen it next to (or on top of) a heating vent in a cardboard box. If the lamb is very cold, immerse its body in a tub of warmish water and, after it loosens up, dry it thoroughly. Though this will rapidly warm the lamb, it has the obvious disadvantage of lessening the bond between ewe and lamb: the lamb will be separated from the ewe while it's in the tub or house, and its distinct odor and taste will become less recognizable to the ewe.

Ultimately, however, your lamb needs to be warmed from within, and that means getting it food. Give the lamb a squirt of warm lamb-saver gel (if you haven't already) and try holding the lamb right up to a teat and even easing a teat into its mouth. The ewe may not be overly cooperative with this procedure, so a second person to hold the ewe is helpful. You can also try holding the ewe down on her side and lying the lamb against her udder, though the ewe is likely to resist this indignity with vigor. But getting the lamb to suckle from its mother is definitely your primary objective.

Your second choice is to feed the lamb from a bottle. If the ewe is producing colostrum, milk some out and put it in a bottle for the lamb. If the ewe is not producing, mix up some instant colostrum—or better yet, thaw out some colostrum that you previously milked from another ewe and froze. Slather the liquid around the nipple so that the lamb can get a taste of it, and slightly squeeze the bottle to pressurize the milk as the lamb suckles. The lamb may not immediately go for this rubber teat; if not, it's OK to slather milk around the nipple and onto the lamb's mouth and face. With luck, the lamb will slowly realize that food is just a mouthful away.

The most difficult scenario is when a lamb just won't suckle and, over time, becomes too weak and cold to even try. At this point, you need to inject warm colostrum directly into the lamb's stomach via a tube. If this sounds invasive, it is. But it's what you need to do to save the lamb's life. The good news is that you won't need to do this more than once or twice for a lamb. After it's received its first good charge of energy via the tube, it will trust you more and will either start taking the bottle or be strong enough to tackle momma directly.

Use a special *lamb-saver kit* especially designed for this purpose. The kit consists of a plastic syringe and a plastic tube. Mix or thaw some colostrum, warm it to body temperature, and fill the syringe to the one-ounce mark. Attach the tube and allow some of the liquid to leak out the tip of the tube, rubbing the liquid along the outside of the tube to lubricate it.

Work the tip of the tube into the corner of the lamb's mouth and push it in a few centimeters until it's snug against the back of the lamb's mouth. The lamb will start to gag and attempt to swallow the tube. Apply gentle pressure at this point so that the tube slides down the esophagus as the lamb gags on it. Once you're past the back of the throat, the lamb will relax again. Slide in about six more inches of tube (enough for the tip to reach down into the stomach) and slowly inject the colostrum into the lamb, taking a minute to empty the whole syringe. When you're done, just pinch the tube closed and slowly pull the tube back out.

The main risk of using the tube is that it could end up going down the trachea into the lungs instead of down the esophagus into the stomach. If you inject liquid at that point, the lamb will drown. The key is to apply slight pressure as the lamb gags when the tube reaches the back of its

mouth. The lamb instinctively wants to swallow the tube, not breath it in, so all will go well as long as you don't force the tube too hard and fast during the gag reflex.

 Above: Parkson, a Navajo-Churro ram lamb, grazes alongside his mother, Tank, at The Land & Lamb Co.

Don't worry: you'll do this if you need to. The very first lamb born at our place was a singleton born to a first-time yearling ewe. As bad luck would have it, I was gone at the time and arrived home about an hour after he had been born. Though the ewe had dried the little fellow off, she had not bonded with him and was not letting him near her somewhat small udder. He was trembling and cold when I spotted his ears sticking up out of a tuft of grass at the edge of the barnyard.

We tried holding him to his mother's teats, but she kicked wildly and would have none of it. We tried giving him a bottle, but he was too weak to take it. Finally, in desperation, I tore open a lamb-saver kit without pausing to read the instructions. I filled the syringe full of colostrum, stuffed the tube down his throat with considerable force, and immediately injected the whole thing into him.

His eyes quickly rolled back into his head, and I was sure I'd killed him. He didn't move. Pausing now to read the instructions on the package, I was horrified to think that I had undoubtedly flooded his lungs with milk. But though he didn't move a muscle, he continued to breathe, and slowly his body started to warm up and relax. After about two hours, his eyelids flickered open, he jumped up, and he was well on his way to being one of the funniest and feistiest lambs we've ever had. Molé was his name; he was a beautiful chocolate brown.

I do think, however, that I got lucky. Take your time easing the tube down the lamb's throat, and take your time easing the liquid into him. Though your task is urgent, you don't want to rush the job.

Phase Three—Sending the Lambs on Their Way

Your ewe and her lambs will want to spend one to three days together in their jug. If it's late in the lambing season, the bond between ewes and lambs has solidified, and your ewe is eager to rejoin her comrades, twenty-four hours may be sufficient. If you have a first-time mom with smallish lambs and no need to spring them from the jug right away, up to three days is fine. Either way, use this period of confinement to check that all is well with the ewe and lambs. It will never be this easy again to give the family a good looking over.

Usually within an hour or two of birth, the ewe will expel the placenta. (She may attempt to eat it, which is fine. If she doesn't, scoop up the placenta and store it in an open container until you have a chance to dispose of it in the woods or dump. If you seal it up inside something, you'll be treated to an unforgettable aromatic assault.) Once the placenta has passed, there should be no more tissue hanging out of the ewe's vulva, and though there will be dried blood on her hind end and udder for a week or so, you should not see any fresh blood or bleeding after the placenta has passed. If there continues to be fresh blood leaking from the vulva after twenty-four hours, call the vet.

Check the ewe's udder daily while she's in the jug to make sure there are no hard lumps or masses in it. If there are, vigorous massage may loosen up the lumps and restore even milk flow throughout the udder. Also, manually milk each teat once or twice to be sure that each teat has milk and that the milk is smooth and a somewhat clear white. We have one ewe that grows an enormous right teat during the last few days of her pregnancy. It's so big that the lambs often fail to recognize it as a teat. I make a point of milking this teat for a minute or so several times a day to reduce its size until the lambs clue in and can take over.

The main risk to ewes during the early weeks of pregnancy is *mastitis*, or inflammation of the udder. The primary symptoms are an obviously red and inflamed udder, an udder that is unusually hot to the touch, lots of lumps in the udder, and/or milk that is very yellow or lumpy. The usual cause of mastitis is too much milk production caused by the ewe eating too much grain or the lambs not being able to keep up with the milk supply. Other causes include an infection creeping in through a teat or a blow or injury to the udder. If you suspect that a ewe has mastitis, call the vet. Leaving it untreated can, at the very least, make it unlikely that your ewe will ever be able to produce milk again.

Monitor the lambs while they are in the jug to make sure they are drinking milk successfully. Assuming that each lamb has passed the cold-mouth, failure-to-stretch, and hunched-back tests, an easy way for you to keep track of them thereafter is by noticing how much they baa. A ewe and her lambs will baa and nicker back and forth every now and again, just to reassure one another and make small talk. The lamb may also baa a few times if it's looking for a teat and will usually wander over and suckle shortly thereafter. A lamb that baas and baas without successfully suckling is a lamb that is becoming hungry and desperate. Try holding the ewe in place and nudging the lamb toward a teat.

 Above: A Suffolk lamb licks its leg while in the pasture. A lamb with a long tail is susceptible to attracting maggots and flies.

Lambs will sleep most of the time during their first twenty-four hours. You shouldn't be alarmed by that or force them to eat unless they are obviously too cold and starved to get up. A lamb that is asleep and breathing smoothly is almost certainly OK. If you're not convinced, check for a cold mouth. You'll soon become proficient at slipping a pinky into a sleeping lamb's mouth without waking it.

One year, one of our ewes had twins, and whenever I went into the barn to check on her, I only saw her licking and nursing one of the lambs. It was always the same lamb: the second was invariably asleep. I grew concerned. But when I finally roused the sleeper and checked for cold mouth, he was fine. It was just my timing that was bad.

At about the twenty-four-hour mark following birth, and before you release the lambs from the jug, you should dock their tails. That means cut them off. Many novice shepherds are horrified by this prospect, which seems both cruel and unnatural. That was certainly my perspective, and one that I shared with our shearer in the spring before our first lambing season. He replied, "There's nothing natural about a sheep walking around with a dozen pounds of wool on it, and nothing natural about a sheep with a wooly tail. Natural's got nothing to do with it. Unless you want to watch your lambs walking around with tails covered by maggots and flies, cut the tails off."

Or something like that. His speech made a great impression on me, and I've been docking tails since year one with no regret. Even sheep that have been bred primarily for meat over the years still have more wool than required for life in the wild.

I've found that docking the tails right at the twenty-four-hour mark is optimal. Prior to that, the lambs are still barely able to stand, so giving them yet another new challenge seems unwise. Much beyond twenty-four hours, the nerves in their tails are developing quickly, and the procedure seems to bother them more and more.

You have two choices for how to dock a lamb's tail. The procedure I use is to slide a special Elastrator rubber band around the tail that constricts blood flow and causes the tail to fall off about three weeks later. The other procedure is to use specially designed pliers that crush the tail and cut it off, after which you need to stitch the wound closed. The advantage of the rubber band is that it is quick and requires no stitching afterwards. That's the route I recommend you go, at least for your first few years.

Where you place the band on the tail is important. Hold the lamb up so that you can clearly see where the tail meets the body. (Having a helper hold the lamb is ideal.) There may be some creamy, peanut-butter-colored poop smeared around the anus by now, which you should clean up with a towel to clear your sight lines. (The poop will change to the more familiar dark pellets by the end of the first week.) As you hold the tail away from the body, notice that there are two flaps of skin that connect the tail to the body on either side of the anus. These are called the *caudal tail flaps*. Your goal is to place the rubber band about a quarter inch beyond where these two flaps meet the tail, leaving a quarter inch of tail remaining below the

 Above: The author holds an Elastrator, designed to loop a rubber band around a lamb's tail for docking. Docking the lamb's tail at the twenty-four-hour mark is optimal.

two flaps ("below" meaning closer to the end of the tail, farther from the body). Any higher up and you will be affecting the two caudal flaps, which may complicate the healing process and create unnecessary discomfort. If placed much lower down, the final tail will hang in the way of the anus.

Once you've released the rubber band onto the tail, open the Elastrator tool again to easily slide it down off the tail. The lamb will undoubtedly squirm and try to see what has happened to its tail. But at the twenty-four-hour mark, the procedure seems to cause more hassle than pain. I've noticed that after several minutes of rapid tail wagging, the lamb relaxes and the discomfort subsides. Give the lamb at least an hour or two in the jug to become familiar with the new tail arrangement and to calm down before releasing ewe and lambs back into the flock.

A second question to contend with at this point is whether or not to castrate any ram lambs. Rams can be castrated at any time in their lives, but doing so when they are small is both less painful and easier to accomplish. Disclaimer: I have never done this, because I've never been sure at such an early point which ram lambs are likely to be sold as breeders and which are likely to head for the freezer. For the ram lambs headed for the freezer, there is no advantage to having them castrated—unless you want to keep them in with your ewes without the risk of unwanted pregnancy. You have enough going on as it is right now, so my advice is to avoid castrating your rams at this point unless you have a good reason to.

If you do decide to castrate your lambs, you can use the Elastrator bands for this job too. Once the ram lamb is roughly three weeks old, you'll be able to feel that his testicles have descended from his body and are now hanging in the scrotum. (Compare him with a younger lamb so that you know what an empty scrotum feels like.) Slide the rubber band up the scrotum so that the testicles are isolated from the body, and release the band. The testicles should fall off in three to four weeks and your ram will be castrated.

Once the tails are docked and the new family is released into the herd, you're pretty much home free. Provided a lamb isn't obviously in trouble or baaing incessantly with no relief, you can assume that all is well. Just keep an eye on things and relish the joy of being a shepherd.

THE BOTTLE LAMB

Every now and again, you will need to raise a lamb yourself by nursing it from a bottle. There can be many reasons for this: the ewe died during delivery, the runt of a triplet litter is getting shut out from the udder, the ewe has mastitis or isn't producing milk, or the initial bonding of lamb and ewe didn't take (this rarely happens but is most common with first-time ewes).

Most shepherds will roll their eyes if you tell them you have a bottle lamb because of the amount of extra work this will entail. Basically, you will need to feed the lamb every day for two months or so, until the lamb is well established on grain or pasture. At first, you should feed a small amount of milk—two to three ounces—every four hours around the clock. Little lambs can't drink enough at one time to last them very long. After four days, go to six ounces every eight hours. Once the lamb is eating solid food in the creep, you can cut this back to one or two full bottles a day or set up a milk bucket with a nipple that allows the lamb continuous access to milk.

We've only had one bottle lamb so far—Molé, the one I nearly drowned with the feeding tube back in year one. Though I dreaded the thought of all the work involved in raising him as a bottle lamb, I found that I actually enjoyed the experience very much and keep secretly hoping we'll have another bottle lamb some day. Whenever I went into the barn with a bottle that year, the little guy would come squirting out of the flock like a watermelon seed and leap into my arms. He loved having his neck scratched while working the bottle, and I enjoyed having such an enthusiastic friend. Lambs are normally quite reticent and will only let their curiosity get the better of them after you've been sitting still in the pen for a while.

If you do end up with a bottle lamb, buy some instant sheep milk replacer and follow the instructions for the proper dosage. It's hard for a bottle lamb to get too much milk in the early days, so you can pretty much

Opposite: A Border Leicester Southdown bottle lamb roams around the barnyard during Open Barn Day at Fat Rooster Farm. The ram lamb became a bottle lamb because his mother stopped nursing him after he fell out of the jug.

give as much as it will drink in one sitting. (Though if the lamb ends up with diarrhea, you're giving too much.) Baby bottles and nipples work fine for this, though buying a specially shaped ewe nipple that attaches to a standard soda bottle is even better. Smear some milk on the nipple the first few times to help the lamb associate it with food, and even squeeze some milk right into the lamb's mouth if needed. After a few feedings, the hungry lamb will never have to be coaxed again.

If you have several bottle lambs, or can't be on hand every few hours for a feeding, you can buy special pails with nipples attached that allow the lamb to drink as needed. The advantage of this, of course, is convenience. The disadvantage is that, over time, the other lambs in the flock will overcome their distrust of milk from a fake nipple and start to pony up themselves. You'll end up feeding relatively expensive milk replacer to the whole crop.

In hindsight, the funniest moment from our bottle lamb year came late in the spring when the lambs were out in a pasture surrounded by portable electric fencing. I was giving Molé one bottle a day at that point, to supplement his grazing and help him keep up with his cousins. I stepped over the electric fence late in the afternoon wearing a T-shirt, sweaty from a day of work on the farm. All lambs—bottle or not—have the instinct to punch the ewe's udder with their noses to stimulate milk production; as I crouched down on my haunches with the bottle, Molé's pokes would occasionally knock me back a step or two and cause me to lose my balance.

I had, of course, forgotten all about the electric fence behind me until one of his pokes pushed my sweaty back against the electrified netting. Since my rubber boots prevented the current from exiting through my feet, it all went out through the bottle into unsuspecting Molé. The bottle shot out of my hand and landed about twenty feet away, and he traveled through the air at least six feet before hitting the ground and galloping to the far end of the pasture, where he hid underneath a tree in disbelief. I myself was sprawled face down in the weeds wondering if I'd just been struck by lightning.

I thought I'd weaned the poor guy for sure. But by the next morning, he was right back to his usual self and resumed poking the milk bottle with unabated enthusiasm. No permanent injuries were reported by either party.

THE FIRST MONTH: EAR TAGS, VACCINES, & DE-WORMER

By the end of their first month of life, you will want to de-worm your lambs, give them their first vaccine, and outfit them with ear tags. I'll talk more about the de-worming and vaccines in chapter 9 on the health of your sheep; but I will give you information about ear tags here.

 Above: Twin Navajo-Churro ewe lambs Spring and Equinox chew their cuds in the barnyard at The Land & Lamb Co. Ear tags are helpful in keeping track of sheep, even in a small flock.

Technically, you don't need ear tags, especially if you are buying spring lambs from someone else for your own consumption or if your lambs are never going to leave your farm (to be shown at the county fair, for example, or to be sold to someone else). If you're sure that your lambs are yours forever, skip the next paragraph.

Otherwise, you should buy a set of numbered ear tags and a tag applicator for attaching them to your lambs' ears. I only raise one to two dozen lambs per year; but even at that small number, I can easily lose track of who is who—especially in the early summer when lambs out on pasture start camouflaging their distinctively colored birth marks beneath

 Above: Gany, a Navajo-
Churro ewe lamb, eats hay
in the creep.

emerging adult wool. A quick check of an ear tag
can confirm—either for you or for a prospective
buyer—that this indeed was the twin born in
March and not the singleton born in early April, or it's the one from your
prized ewe and not the one from the yearling.

Attaching an ear tag is very straightforward. Load the tag into the
applicator pliers, have someone hold the lamb's head for you, find a nice
clear spot in the middle of the ear, and quickly squeeze the pliers to punch
the tag through the ear and into its backer plate. Quickly release the tag from
the applicator, and watch the lamb prance comically around the pen with
one ear up and the other weighted down by the tag. Despite their surprise
at no longer being level-headed, the lambs don't seem unduly put out by
the operation: there must not be many nerve endings in those leathery ears.

There are two ways to go wrong here, although that isn't many in the grand scheme of things. First, don't buy ear tags designed for calves; your poor lambs will end up dragging their weighted ears along the ground. Second, make sure that the tags you use are designed to work with the tag applicator you have. There are about three distinct tag types out there, each of which works only with its specific applicator. I discovered the difference one year when, in a brilliant bid to save a few bucks, I borrowed a tag applicator from one friend to use with extra tags I'd been given by another. While a half dozen of my family members looked on, I confidently squeezed the first tag into the first lamb's ear only to have the thing misalign with the backer plate and end up halfway stuck through the now-bleating lamb's ear. By the time I separated the tag and applicator from the gyrating lamb, I was quite convinced that my family was going to wrestle me to the ground and force a tag through my own ear just to see how much I liked it. I haven't made that mistake again.

You also need to give your lambs a CD/T vaccine sometime in their first month of life, followed by a booster shot four weeks later. See chapter 9 on healthcare for full details on how to do this. Since lambs tend to be born over a two- to three-week period, I usually wait until the youngest is two weeks old or so and then vaccinate the whole crop.

Lambs also need to be de-wormed, because they are more susceptible to serious worm infestations than ewes and rams are. The two logical times to do this are when the lambs start grazing and eating fresh pasture and when they are weaned. Depending on your lambing schedule, these two events may be happening at the same time. If not, you may want to de-worm them both times (see chapter 9 for more on the details on de-worming).

NAMING YOUR LAMBS

I'll come clean here: I name my lambs. Every year. Even the ones I know I'm going to eat.

I usually pick some sort of theme for the names, which helps me remember one year from the next. The first year it was Spanish names; we had Luna, Noche, Molé—in honor of their Navajo-Churro heritage. The next it was dwarves from *The Hobbit*; Dori, Nori, and Ori were the triplets, thanks to the Tolkien craze that was sweeping the land that year. Last year it was presidents and first ladies (Dwight and Mamie were my favorite pairing), in keeping with the nation's quadrennial election obsession.

The way I look at it, I'm going to know each lamb individually no matter what, and it feels more honest to apply a name to a lamb rather than pretend that "ear tag #23" somehow keeps us at arm's length. Plus, everyone who visits our farm wants to know what the lambs' names are. Telling them, "That's the white one with the brown spots, the twin from ewe #12" doesn't get you far with the kindergarten set. Our smallest lamb last year was a black singleton we named Eleanor—very small, black, and distinctive among the milling flock. Kids were shrieking "Eleanor!" in delight all summer as they ran around the farm. I wouldn't want to have missed that.

THE FIRST MONTH: THE CREEP

As soon as you've named your lambs (or not!), you should start thinking about setting up a creep for them. A creep is simply a place where lambs can go but adults can't—so when the time comes, you can put out extra food for the lambs, or catch them for a vaccination, or just generally check on their well-being. I usually take the panels that comprise the lambing jugs and reorient them to make the creep. The key detail, of course, is the doorway into the creep. This needs to be large enough for the lambs to squeeze through yet small enough and strong enough to keep the ewes out, since they will make a concerted effort to gain access. The yearling ewes (the ones that are now in their second year of life) are particularly persistent; they fit through the very same door last year and can't understand why they are now being kept away from the fun.

I make a little doorway by screwing together scrap lumber and find that inside dimensions of nine inches wide by twenty inches high work well for my Navajo-Churro lambs, which are smaller than some breeds. As with your main sheep pen, solid walls will help the lambs feel more comfortable in the creep, as will plenty of light and air. Build some sort of grain feeder about a foot off the floor, and you're all set.

I know I spoke earlier about the importance of not feeding grain to sheep, but I make an exception for lambs in their first ten to twelve weeks of life. Lambs are growing so fast that they aren't wasting the extra calories on body fat, and I find the extra charge of nutrition helps the lambs gain strength and vigor during their vulnerable early months. Within two weeks of the first lambs being born, I'll put a little bit of grain into the creep feeder and watch the lambs nuzzle and pretend to eat it. Watching lambs pretend to eat grain and hay—all proud of themselves for being a grown-up just like mom—is sidesplitting entertainment. A single stalk of grass can occupy a lamb for five or ten minutes or more, slowly going back and forth through the lamb's soft mouth without sustaining the slightest damage.

But play-feeding also serves an important purpose: the sooner the lambs start ingesting solid food, the sooner their rumens will "turn on" and enable them to start gaining weight with enthusiasm. Allowing this process to commence naturally—a few kernels of grain here, the odd blade of grass there—is both the quickest and safest way for the lambs to transition to their adult diet. There's some evidence that the sooner a lamb starts eating solid food, the larger and healthier it will grow in adulthood.

THE SECOND MONTH: WEANING

By the end of their second month, your lambs will be eating grain with abandon. I usually give them roughly a quarter pound of grain per lamb per day, which is pretty close to all they can eat. Between that and continued access to momma's milk, your lambs will be growing like weeds.

This raises the question: how long should they continue to nurse from their mothers? From the lambs' perspective, as long as possible; all calories are good. But from the ewes' perspective, the thrill starts to wane after a few months, especially once the lambs are so large that they—quite literally—lift their mothers' hindquarters off the ground when they race in to nurse. From your perspective, most of your ewes will be scoring in the 2 range at this point—after having spent all spring growing and feeding lambs. They could use some time off over the summer to recover their strength.

In the wild, of course, lambs would be slowly weaned over the course of the summer. But you will want to choose a set date, particularly if you have ram lambs that will need to be removed from their mothers as they sexually mature. The trick with weaning is not to do it cold turkey. If your lambs are suddenly removed from their mothers, the ewes' udders are apt to become so full of unwanted milk that they become inflamed and infected (mastitis). Time to call the vet to get you set up administering antibiotics.

Instead, you want the process of weaning to unfold gradually. For about forty-eight hours, keep your flock penned up in the barnyard. Feed your ewes a minimal amount of water and as much dry hay as they want. (Here's your chance to finish up those extra few bales from last winter; old, brown hay without much moisture and nutrition is what you're looking for here, not anything green and fresh.) You want to deprive the ewes of milk-building nutrients without shutting down their rumens altogether. During this time, the lambs will continue suckling from their mothers, helping to drain the udders of their dwindling milk supply.

After forty-eight hours, remove the lambs from the ewes and keep them separate for at least the next two weeks. Keep the lambs as far away from the ewes as possible: the sound of a crying lamb is enough to stimulate a ewe to continue producing milk. (It's also enough to stimulate a shepherd to wear ear plugs, borrow a muffler-less leaf blower, or rent a motel room far away in order to get some sleep.) I've worked out a great arrangement with the friends who sold me my original flock. I load the lambs into our pickup truck and drive them over to their place, where the old pens and fences are still set up and available for use. The lambs spend two weeks together over there, usually with hardly a bleat of protest once they settle in.

Your ewes, however, will definitely mount a protest, even if they can't hear their lambs. Keep them in the barnyard on their low-cal, low-water, brown-hay diet for the next four days or so, checking their udders twice per day to see how they are doing. After the first day, their udders will likely be full and warm. By the end of the second day, they will still be full but hopefully not quite so tight and warm. After three days or so, they should have started to noticeably soften as the milk inside starts to be

reabsorbed. After a month or so, the udders will be nearly gone—retracted back up under the ewes' bellies with only the enlarged teats to prove they once held milk.

 Above: A Romney Southdown ewe leads her ewe lamb out to pasture for the first time at Fat Rooster Farm.

This is the ideal case, of course, which not all of your ewes will be able to pull off. Some udders will remain hot and tight for several days; others, more typically, will soften on one side but not on the other. Your task with these ewes is to milk them a little bit—enough to relieve their discomfort but not so much that you drain the udder completely; doing so will only stimulate the ewe to produce more milk. Do your best to massage out any lumps that you might feel in an udder, being careful not to poke the udder the way lambs do to let down more milk.

If an udder refuses to cool off and drain, and especially if it becomes warmer by the day or starts to feel solid and hard, you've got mastitis on your hands. Either intervene with antibiotics, if you know what you're doing, or call the vet right away. At a minimum, untreated mastitis will destroy the udder's ability to produce milk; in the worst case, the infection can spread throughout the ewe and kill her.

Assuming you've avoided any mastitis, and once you're comfortable that all the udders are noticeably starting to reduce in size, gradually reintroduce either better hay or fresh pasture to your ewes after roughly four days. Just as you do in springtime, let them fill up on dry hay before you introduce the good stuff, and limit their pasture to a few hours a day for the first few days until their rumens recharge. After that, you're in the clear and so are they.

THE INEVITABLE DEATH

I was well into my third lambing season before I lost my first lamb. That year, one of my first-time ewes gave birth to triplets, one of which never made it out of its amniotic sac and died. It might have been stillborn to begin with, or it might have struggled and failed. Either way, I wasn't home to see it or do anything about it.

As you might expect, I felt nauseous and negligent for having been away from the farm at the crucial hour. I had vowed, back when I first bought my flock, that I would do everything right and never lose a lamb. But I now know that such a vow is not possible to keep; you simply can't be on hand for every birth. You just need to do the best you can, learn from your mistakes, improve your systems for the next time, and recognize that with sheep—as with all animals (humans included)—death is inextricably linked with life. You could give up shepherding altogether, but then all the wonderful lambs who would have been born at your farm will never get that chance.

What should you do with a dead lamb's carcass? If you live in a rural area with lots of land, leaving the body in the woods for other critters to eat is the simplest and easiest approach—and you will make some carnivore's day. But if that carnivore happens to be a coyote—and nearly all of us live in coyote territory these days—you may not want to familiarize your local canines with the taste of lamb. Wrapping the carcass in a plastic bag and taking it to your local dump is also a good option, as is burying it a few feet down in the ground or buring it inside a compost pile.

A FINAL NOTE: KNOW YOUR SHEEP

During lambing, as is the case throughout the year, it pays for you to have a sense of what "normal" is for your animals. For example, one year our normally reclusive ewe Ramona, who had been in labor for a few hours and seemed to be struggling mightily, came over to the rail where I was standing, looked me straight in the eye, and let out an enormous "baahhhhh." I jumped into the pen, gave her a hand, and fifteen minutes later she was licking her newly born twins with enthusiasm.

If Clover had let out that mighty "baahhhhh," I probably would have rubbed her behind the ears and let her keep circling for a while. Clover is always coming up to me in the barn and baaing for attention and affection: she's a social sponge. Ramona, on the other hand, is the wariest of our sheep: she rarely has anything to say and never approaches me or volunteers information. One time she sprained an ankle and hobbled around on three legs for a few days, all the while doing a pretty good job of keeping away from me. So when Ramona came to the rail and baacd in my face, I knew it was time to swing into action.

CHAPTER EIGHT
Shearing and Wool

Shearing day is one of my favorite days on the
sheep calendar. Wooly, heavy-looking animals
trundle in one side and skinny, skittish animals jump
out the other. In the middle, each sheep is liberated from
its fleece as if being unzipped from a sleeping bag.

But "sleeping bag" doesn't begin to describe the beautiful, luxurious fleece
that's left after the sheep regains its feet and darts off to rejoin the flock. You'll
want to sink both hands into the warm, deep wool, and bury your nose in the
rich lanolin. I confess that I've never been a spinner, and only once a knitter;
but when that first sheep jumps out of its fleece and leaves its wonderful wool
behind, I want to drop everything and devote my career to the woolen arts.

A typical fleece can weigh up to a dozen pounds or so. On a roughly 150-
pound adult sheep, this comes to well less than ten percent of its total
weight. But the startling aspect of sheepshearing is that the fleece can be
fifty percent or more of the animal's volume. When the last of the wool falls
away beneath the shears, your sheep may be only half the size it was just a
few minutes earlier.

As soon as the shearer releases a shorn sheep, it will inevitably jump up,
run over to rejoin the rest of the flock, and then turn to cast a sidelong
glance back toward you. Be sure to
notice this sidelong glance: my wife
insists this is where the adjective
sheepish comes from, and I'm inclined
to agree with her. There's a blending of
embarrassment, nudity, bewilderment,

Opposite: Navajo-Churro ewes
Crepe, in foreground, and Bragg
graze at a neighbor's pasture in
Tunbridge, Vermont. Owner Marian
White brings the sheep into the
barn at night.

 Above: Yarn from Marian White's Navajo-Churro sheep, both dyed and natural in color, is ready for knitting.

and defiance that you rarely get to see in the legal sectors of the economy.

Observers of shearing at our farm often blurt out "Poor thing!" at least once during the proceedings as a sheepish animal jostles its way back into the fold. Especially for the first few animals, being shorn makes them both smaller and somewhat unrecognizable to the rest of the flock, so be prepared for some jostling and shoving as the "new" animals return to the group. This will die down as the

shorn gain the majority. And while the tendency to view a shorn animal as a poor thing may be strong, keep in mind that after several millennia of being bred to carry ever-greater quantities of wool, sheep may be happier than you think to be rid of their ten-pound coats.

Part of my joy on shearing day stems from the fact that I don't shear the sheep myself. I hire a pro. He comes to our farm and does the technical work while I help out with the handling of the wool and the sheep. You, however, may want to do the shearing yourself, especially if you only have a few sheep. If that's the route you choose, more power to you; I'm sure it'll be a great adventure. Being able to bend at the waist and touch your toes, however, is an essential attribute of the successful sheepshearer: I last touched my toes in late 1999, and that was only after an extended year-long stretching campaign. I have too much back and too little hamstring to ever hit the big time as a sheepshearer.

Plus, it's fun to have a sheepshearer around the place. Our shearer, in addition to shearing the sheep, offers up a continuous stream of good suggestions for how to upgrade our fencing, save money, keep the sheep healthy, and generally improve the operation. At the same time, he deals from an apparently inexhaustible deck of off-color and political jokes, which makes it easier to accept the fact that some guy has come onto our farm and pointed out all the mistakes and dumb things we've been doing.

Besides, there's plenty of work to do before, during, and after shearing—even if you aren't the person wielding the shears. Do what you can to have a few friends on hand to help with the details. I used to think it was an imposition asking people to help out, but as the same family and friends have turned out year after year to help on shearing day, I've come to realize that all but the most jaded people get caught up in the magic and humor of watching fully grown animals jump out of their skins.

WHEN TO SHEAR

If you have pregnant ewes, the best time to shear them is two to four weeks before your first possible lambing date. A recently shorn ewe is both easier for you to observe as she goes into labor and more likely to give birth inside your barn or shelter, where the lamb will be less exposed to the elements. If she's warm and toasty under her ten-pound fleece, she may overlook the fact that her lamb will not be.

Otherwise, spring and fall are the best seasons for shearing, though you can shear your sheep most anytime if needed. They will certainly appreciate not being shorn in the middle of January in a cold northern climate, but if your barn is tight and not too drafty, they'll be OK. Similarly, they'd much rather be shorn before the heat of summer sets in. Our flock here in central Vermont seems much more put out on a ninety-degree afternoon than on a twenty-below morning, so we aim to have them shorn every spring.

Finally, if you have an especially long-wooled breed and want to have your wool commercially spun into yarn, you may want to shear your sheep twice a year. Commercial spinning machines have trouble with wool that is longer than four inches, so shearing twice per year will solve this problem. Hand-spinners, however, love to work with long wool. But since shearing does cost money, you'll probably want to stick with once per year unless your wool market demands otherwise.

WOOL CONSIDERATIONS

Some people raise sheep exclusively for their wool. Others raise sheep for meat, or grounds-keeping, or some combination of the above. This decision

will determine how much care you should put into your wool prior to shearing day.

Above: Bruce Wooster moves Desdemona into place at Sunrise Farm, while shearer Andy Rice stretches before starting the annual clipping.

Wool that fetches the highest price per pound is clean, neat, and free of sticks, burrs, pieces of hay or straw, or poop. Since your sheep live in a world full of such stuff, this is easier said than done. My sheep emerge from a summer and autumn of grazing out in the pastures with wool that is nearly perfectly clean and ready for sale as is. After a winter in the barn, however, the opposite is true: their wool is clogged with leftover hay and bedding. The key to clean wool is to make your winter conditions match your summer conditions.

First and foremost, try to feed your hay so your animals have to bend down to eat it—as if they were grazing. Place your feeder only a foot or so off the ground; if you end up tossing the hay into the feeder from above, be sure the chaff won't fall onto the heads and necks of your sheep on its way into the feeder. Also, make sure your sheep have ample room at the feeder. This way, when your sheep step back with a mouthful of hay for some contemplative chewing, they aren't so crowded that they end up eating over the backs of their neighbors.

Second, use straw as the topmost layer of bedding in your barn or shelter. The long, tough stalks in straw are less apt to become lodged in fleece compared to sawdust, wood shavings, or hay—and they are much easier to pick out if they do. Hay or sawdust are great as an underlayer for absorption, but using straw on top will help keep your fleeces clean.

Finally, you can make or buy jackets for your sheep to protect their fleeces—which will keep them clean and make the fleece denser. If you are in the high-end wool business, this is far and away the best way to keep your wool in pristine condition. For the rest of us, however, the expense and hassle of dressing sheep for success is probably not worth it. And in the interest of full disclosure, I should mention that my wife and I are Standard Poodle owners. We have a hard-enough time justifying this to our fellow farmers, and the conversation would only get more involved and difficult if we were also dressing our sheep in jackets.

You may be raising sheep not for their wool but for their meat, their grass-cutting expertise, or the simple joy of their company. In that case, don't get too worked up about the cleanliness of their wool. Unless there are bird's nests or raspberry canes in your fleeces, your shearer won't be overly put out. It may seem sacrilegious to say this, but one of the most cost-effective ways for dealing with the wool that your sheep grow (in this age of synthetic fleece and fossil-fuel clothing) is to let it get as dirty as it gets and throw it away after shearing. I'm convinced that far more money has been lost by the shepherds who "add value" to their wool without having a market for it than by those who simply haul their fleeces into the woods and let the birds and rodents believe they've won the nest-building lottery.

PREPARING FOR SHEARING DAY

Several months before your proposed shearing day, book your shearer. Though there are far fewer sheep in the world than there once were, there are even fewer shearers—and they are often hard to get. Find the name of a reputable shearer in your area and line him or her up several months in advance.

Next, round up a supply of family and friends to help you with the 10,000 details of shearing a sheep. You can easily put three or four people to work opening and closing gates, separating sheep from the flock, gathering up the wool, and sweeping up poop and debris.

Third, figure out how you are going to handle the fleeces as they come off of the animals. I usually wrap an old bedsheet around each fleece and tie up the corners, though you can also buy special fleece bags for this purpose. You don't want to use any synthetic grain or feed bags: any plastic fibers that find their way into the fleece will drive the spinner to distraction. Don't use plastic trash bags either, because the wool will give off moisture as it cools and will mold or rot if wrapped in plastic. However you handle the fleeces, make sure it's quick and efficient; they'll be plenty of time to ooh and aah over the wool later on when the shearer isn't on the meter and hovering over you.

Fourth, the shearer is going to want to stand in a clean, dry place to do the shearing, so figure out these logistics in advance. Rather than arrange a way to get the sheep out of their pen and into a clean spot, I find it easier to bring a clean tarp or, better yet, a sheet of plywood right into the pen and lay it down to create a clean zone. The shearer and fleece will stay on the board or tarp while you stay on the pen floor with the sheep. Unless your shearer is trying to show off his skills with hand shears, you'll also need to have an extension cord or outlet handy for plugging in the electric shearing motor.

Finally, your sheep will need to be dry on shearing day, so keep them out of the rain, dew, or fog for at least forty-eight hours prior to shearing. There is almost no way to adequately spread out and dry a wet fleece once it's been shorn off its owner. Plus, the shearer will already have his hands full holding onto the naturally oily sheep without adding water to the mix—which turns your sheep into their cousins, greased pigs. Also, on the morning of shearing day, either go very light on the feed and water or—if you can withstand the invective they will hurl at you—avoid feeding your sheep altogether. Sheep have a tendency to poop and pee in moments of uncertainty, and there will be plenty such moments in the course of being shorn.

HOOVES & SHOTS

Since either you or your shearer is about to have each of your sheep in a fully compromised and cooperative position, seize the opportunity to trim their hooves and administer any vaccines or de-wormers as needed. A shearer will often be happy to perform these services for a small additional fee, so make sure you've purchased the tools and medications in advance or arrange for him or her to bring them along. The annual CD/T vaccine is typically administered during shearing (especially to pregnant ewes) along with some sort of de-wormer and, if needed, a rabies shot. More on all this in the healthcare chapter.

SHEARING DAY

Your prime concern on shearing day should be the efficient handling of your animals. You don't want to be chasing sheep around a distant pasture—and the shearer and your helpers don't want to be watching you do it, either. Move your sheep into their confinement pen before the shearer arrives. If you have a small number of sheep—a dozen or less— you can return each sheep back into the confinement pen after it has been shorn. This gives the sheep the comfort of companionship throughout the process. If you have a larger number of sheep, however, you may find it easier to release the shorn sheep into the larger shelter or outside into the barnyard. This makes it harder on the first and last sheep to be shorn, because they end up being briefly alone; but it's easier on you since you aren't wading in among shorn sheep to cut out the ones still to go.

If you are trying for high-quality wool, shear your sheep in order from lightest to darkest. A few light-colored hairs won't spoil the quality of a dark fleece, but a few dark hairs will definitely mar a light fleece. Between

each shearing, take a broom to quickly clean any wool or debris off of the shearer's clean area to prevent the next fleece from being unnecessarily dirtied. Keep a trash bag or bucket on hand for all this stuff, which will also include the belly wool that your shearer will toss to the side.

 Above: Shearer Andy Rice shaves the belly wool of Navajo-Churro ewe Desdemona at Sunrise Farm. The belly wool is removed first and discarded before the rest of the fleece is taken off in one piece.

Ideally, you should have at least four people at work on shearing day to make it go smoothly: the animal person, whose job it is to secure the next animal to be shorn; the fleece person, whose job is to gather and remove each fleece from the shearing area; the floater, whose job is to open and close gates, sweep up, and generally deal with unexpected contingencies; and the shearer.

Here are two final handling notes. First, never grab and hold your sheep by their wool: it is painful for the sheep, can damage the wool, and can

 Above: Navajo-Churro roving sold by The Land & Lamb Co., ready to be spun.

bruise the animal's skin when the wool pulls on it too tightly. Instead, maneuver your animals around by the horns (if they have them) or by the neck and tail (more on this in the next chapter). Second, take a look at each fleece as it comes off of the animal. Is the wool nice and uniform its entire length? If so, your sheep has had a healthy year since the last shearing. Or is there a weak spot or a distinct break in there somewhere? Grab a hank and pull on it. If it breaks, you're in trouble. Sheep may put insufficient energy into wool production when they are sick or unduly stressed. If all of the fleeces from your flock look good except the one from the animal who needed antibiotics for a hoof injury, now you know why that one fleece has a weak spot, known as "a break in the staple." But if all of your fleeces display that same weakness, however, here's a chance to review your overall management strategy. Maybe you shouldn't have let them go so long without water last summer or fed them such thin rations over the winter.

STORING AND CLEANING WOOL

When the sheep jumps up and runs back to the flock, the fleece left behind will be intact as one big piece. See if you can keep it that way as you initially gather it up and store it in a sheet or burlap sack for later processing. The wool fibers are not attached to each other in any way now that they've been separated from the sheep's skin, so gather up the fleece instead of pulling it and rolling it. This will make life easier later on.

On shearing day, or on any later convenient day, your next job is to *skirt* the fleece. Skirting is simply the process of removing hay and debris from the wool and discarding any matted or low-quality wool, including any of the *second clippings* (very short snippets of wool created when the shearer went back over a previously sheared spot and cut the wool even closer to the body). The best way to do this is to spread the fleece out, with the outside up and the inside (the ends that were nearest the animal's skin) down, on a skirting table.

Your skirting table can be anything from a clean section of floor roughly four feet by eight feet to a specially built skirting table of similar size, made out of slats spread over a frame. The advantage of the raised, slatted table is that you aren't stooping over the fleece and any dirt and debris can drop through to the floor. I haven't built myself a skirting table yet; I just use a four-foot by eight-foot sheet of plywood atop two sawhorses. Whatever you decide to use, keep in mind that it will soon be nicely finished in a fine coating of lanolin—so don't use the kitchen floor.

How good of a skirting job do you need to do? This depends entirely on what you intend to do with the wool. If your eventual market is a hand-spinner, or even the county fair, you want to do a very good job indeed: remove every last piece of hay and chaff and all of the matted and dirt-caked wool from around the edges. (The edges of the fleece are the areas that were closest to the ground, the neck, and the rump.) Keep in mind that the wool will be dirty, which is fine because it will eventually be washed. You just want to get rid of the matted and caked sections that won't be improved even by washing.

I send much of our wool off to a company that turns it into quilt battings, and I only do an average job of skirting each fleece because it is going to end up being mechanically washed and carded. I remove all the big pieces of

 Above: A red knit-lace children's cardigan, a tam, and a blanket are a few of the Shetland wool products for sale at Maple Ridge Sheep Farm.

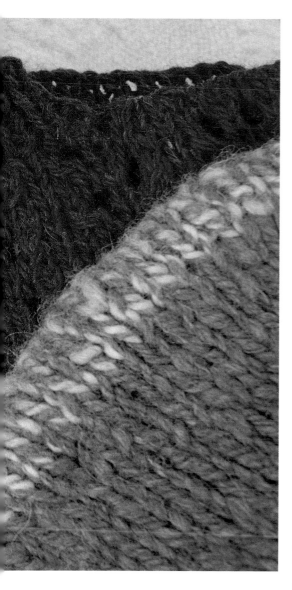

debris and the badly matted areas, but I don't sweat the details too much. Mechanical equipment can remove all kinds of small stuff; you just want to make sure nothing is big and bad enough to get caught in the machines. Plus, there's no point paying to ship several pounds of dirt and debris that are only going to be discarded at the factory.

Once you have skirted a fleece, roll it up for storage. The preferred method for rolling a fleece is to make sure that the best wool ends up on the outside, where you or your buyer can see it, and the lower quality wool ends up safety tucked inside. With the fleece still lying animal-side down, fold the fleece in thirds the long way, fold the neck down onto the back, and then roll the fleece up from the butt to the shoulders and neck. You'll be left looking at the underside of the lovely back wool, since the outside is now in and the inside is now out.

If the fleece is cool and dry, you can store it for short periods in a trash bag. But be sure to keep it out of direct sunlight, which will cause moisture to condense inside the bag. If you're storing fleeces long-term, use burlap, old bedsheets, or some other breathable material. Be sure to label the color and date of the fleece, as well as the sheep's name, so that you don't have to unroll the fleece in future to figure out whose it is.

WHAT TO DO WITH WOOL

There are a hundred and one wonderful things to do with wool, and you are limited only by your imagination. I'll outline just a few of the options.

Use it yourself! If you are handy and crafty, use your wool to make products for your own use or sale. Assuming you have an eventual market for your products (giving gifts is a fine one), this is the most economical way to go since you'll be getting your wool for free. You'll need to wash the wool, dry it, card it, and then either use the rovings (carded sheets of wool) directly for quilting and/or felting or hand-spin it into yarn. Whole books have been written about these various techniques, and I'll leave you in better hands than mine for how best to perform these steps.

An intermediate step is to send your wool out to be washed, dried, carded, and possibly spun; then you can either use it yourself or sell it in its value-added state to interested customers. This angle appeals the most to me since we have a fair number of sheep, and washing, drying, and carding a bunch of fleeces is a more time-consuming enterprise than most people imagine. Unless you love the process, you may be better off spending the money to have the pros process it for you.

Finally, you can sell the unprocessed fleeces as is. If your wool is well suited for hand-spinning and you have some hand-spinners in your area, this is far and away the most financially lucrative approach. A high-quality fleece can fetch five to ten dollars and up per pound from a hand-spinner. But before you start multiplying large sums in your head, keep in mind that a single ten-pound fleece can occupy a casual hand-spinner for years.

You can also sell your wool wholesale to a dealer or buying pool. If you can do this with very little effort on your end, besides a cursory skirting, go for it. But most of these pools pay far less than a buck a pound, and your prep time and the shipping costs will quickly eat up all of that and more. As I mentioned before, unless wool is your passion and your markets are teeming, don't be afraid to throw your wool to the birds. You'll have much more free time to sit on your porch and revel in the pastoral beauty of your sheep farm.

Right: Rugs woven with Navajo-Churro wool show their color and intricacy.

CHAPTER NINE

The Health of Your Sheep

"Yes, but what if they get sick?" That is the question that woke me in the middle of the night just before our first flock arrived on the farm. I was starting to visualize the other parts of the shepherd's routine—the feeding, the fencing, the housing—but I couldn't imagine what I would do in the event of an emergency. I am not a doctor and have little medical knowledge beyond the CPR that most people know. And CPR didn't seem like the sort of skill that was going to get me very far in the world of sheep.

The good news is that ovine medical care is far easier than it first appears. Your sheep want to be healthy just as much as you want them to, so your number one job is simply to make sure they have what they need. Sheep have a widespread reputation for being fragile animals that are always getting sick. Upon learning that I raise sheep, more than one person has said something to the effect of: Sheep are impossible—one minute they're healthy, and the next minute they're lying there dead!

The reason for this misconception is that sheep go out of their way to disguise when they are sick or in distress. In the wild, predators are always on the lookout for sick-looking animals that might make easy targets. Having only their safety-in-numbers tactic to rely on for protection, sheep will go to great lengths to appear inconspicuous when they are in trouble. Therefore, the first place to look for a sick sheep is

Opposite: Jennifer Megyesi drizzles grain on the ground to bring the flock back in through a gate that had blown open at Fat Rooster Farm. Megyesi also works as a veterinary technician, a job that helps her quickly notice problems with animals on her own farm.

not right in front of you—waving its hooves up and down, trying to get your attention—but deep in the middle of your flock, trying to look invisible. If a sheep falls over dead one day, apparently inexplicably, it's not because sheep are especially delicate: it's because you didn't notice when one was sick.

Most of the sheep books I've read have a chapter on medical care that includes an astounding list of sheep maladies and potential cures. The first time I saw one of these lists, I almost called off my life with sheep before it had even started; I couldn't see how I could possibly know enough to be a responsible and capable shepherd.

Now, some years later, I've come to a different conclusion: the list of maladies was the problem, not my lack of veterinary training. Some of these healthcare chapters end up being little more than scare tactics—lists of everything that could possibly go wrong rather than tips for how to treat the easy stuff and clues for when to call the vet. Are human parents expected to identify and treat dozens of human illnesses prior to becoming parents? Of course not: they do what they can and call the doc when they're in over their head. The same should be true for beginning shepherds: learn the basics and know when to call the vet for the rest.

As you gain more experience as a shepherd, especially if you develop a passion for ovine healthcare, you'll find that what you consider to be "basic" will grow larger by the year. The first time I needed to vaccinate my sheep, for example, I called the vet. This turned out to be a great way for me to meet her, for her to meet my sheep, and for me to learn how to wield a vaccination needle. Now I wouldn't dream of calling the vet for a simple CD/T vaccine: that's just basic! But it wasn't basic at the outset—and it needn't be basic for you, either, if you're brand new (as I was) to owning livestock.

But calling the vet every few weeks can get to be an expensive habit, so you have some incentive to learn quickly. There are four areas, it seems to me, that any self-respecting, beginning shepherd should learn to keep an eye on: feed, hooves, worms, and vaccines. Beyond that, most everything else is likely to require a call to the vet, at least when you're starting out. You can always buy a book or two later on devoted exclusively to sheep healthcare and spend your winter evenings in front of the fire looking at the vivid photos and imagining all sorts of doom and gloom for your flock. But by then, you'll be an accomplished shepherd who walks with a swagger and knows that most of these maladies are not worth losing sleep over.

FEED PROBLEMS

The majority of common sheep maladies stem from problems with diet, so feeding your sheep a proper diet is the single most important way to keep them healthy. The chapter on Feeding Your Sheep covers this in some detail, but the general idea is that your sheep's diet should be neither too rich nor too lean, should never change rapidly from one feed to another, and should always include access to either a salt lick or a tray of mineral salt. Free-choice minerals for sheep are like multi-vitamin pills for humans—cheap and easy health insurance. Sheep intuitively know when they need a little selenium, and you will not. What could be easier than letting them choose it as needed?

This brings up the larger point, also mentioned earlier in the book, that it is important to pay attention to your sheep and know what "normal" is. I find that our sheep make very little noise when they are happy campers. They will groan and grunt a bit when given fresh hay, and they will certainly baa back at me in delight if I baa to them while opening a gate to fresh pasture. But if I hear a bunch of baas from the barnyard in the middle of the day, or within minutes of having introduced fresh hay or fresh pasture, I know for sure that something isn't right. The challenge is to figure the problem out quickly, before it becomes a medical problem.

The first summer we had sheep, one of our pasture areas was an old roadway that had been seeded down to a thick bed of white clover. Unlike most of our pastures, where clover is scattered here and there among the grasses, this pasture was probably half clover or more. I loved putting the sheep into this pasture, because I knew they loved clover and clover was a good high-protein food for them.

Well, the first few times I rotated the sheep into the clover pasture, all seemed fine. They did go crazy for it. But as the summer progressed, they seemed to lose their enthusiasm, despite the fact that there was lots of uneaten clover still available. At one point, despite the fact that they were baaing quite frequently, I left them in the clover pasture for nearly a week—for the clover looked so much better than the grasses in the other pastures that were starting to brown up in the mid-summer drought.

By the end of the week, the intrepid Ramona had stopped walking on her left rear leg, and stalwart Desdemona had started favoring a hoof as well. I tried cleaning the hooves but didn't find anything. I started fearing that my flock was developing foot rot, which is a major scourge of sheep. In a panic, I called the vet.

She trimmed the hooves down very close and noticed that the hard outer shells were delaminating and filling with ooze on the affected feet. The diagnosis: laminitis, a problem that is common in ungulates (especially horses) and is brought on by eating a diet too rich in protein. Like white clover.

Oh! The clouds parted. With new eyes, I noticed that my sheep had done their best to eat every green thing in the pasture except the white clover that, due to its predominance, they had nevertheless been forced to eat. All week they had been telling me there was a problem, and all week I had been telling them to shut up and eat the clover, which I "knew" was good for them. It wasn't until I had a hefty vet bill and was changing hoof dressings for a few days that I conceded that the whole episode could have been avoided had I been more observant and less insistent.

The point is: pay attention. If your sheep are telling you they aren't happy, figure out why.

HOOF INJURIES

After diet, hooves are the most common source of problems for sheep. It's easy to see why: to me, their hooves have always seemed too small and fragile for such blocky, bulky animals. Sheep aren't light and nimble like deer or even goats and horses; they are heavy on their feet like cows yet lack the large dinner-plate feet that cows have. My sheep have to climb a small ramp to go from the barnyard to the barn, and I'm always struck while I watch them ascend—or worse, descend—that their hooves are too small for their bodies. Perhaps the millennia we've spent breeding sheep for wool and meat have created this imbalance.

Just as with diet, the key to hoof care is preventative maintenance. Sheep hooves are made of collagen, much like human nails—and like our nails, they continue to grow year-round. You'll need to trim them at least twice a year. I usually have our shearer trim the hooves in the spring during shearing, and then I do a fall trimming myself. Knowing how to trim hooves and having the right tools gives me the confidence to fix any hoof that becomes cracked or damaged at any time.

Trimming hooves isn't particularly hard, but it's not immediately obvious to the uninitiated. There is no substitute here for having a friend, a vet, or a shearer show you the ropes the first few times. The tools are simple—either hoof shears or a hoof knife— and once you get the hang of it, you'll feel like a pro.

The first thing to do is to catch the animal in question by moving the flock into the confinement pen. Next, you want to sit the sheep on its butt. Watch your shearer do this, and you'll notice when a sheep is sitting down, it will cease to struggle and will give in to your demands. To sit a sheep on its butt, approach it from the side, lift its head up, and then push its head away from you until it's bent around over its back and facing its tail. With your other hand, press down on the animal's rump. Ease the rear hips toward you, leaning the animal against your legs. Finally, step slowly backward, using the head to steer the animal down onto either its butt or until it's lying on its side.

Once the sheep is sitting down, have a friend hold the animal upright while you work on the hooves. It's possible but quite challenging to both hold the animal and work on the hooves. Alternatively, you can buy a sheep chair, which is a metal frame with rubber netting that holds the sheep upright and makes this a one-person job (see the appendix on tools and equipment).

For starters, your sheep's hooves are apt to be caked in mud or poop, which you'll need to remove. The easiest way is just to brush or scrape the muck off using the back of the knife or the closed shears. Then you'll

 Above: Andy Rice clips the hooves of Clover before shearing at Sunrise Farm. The key to hoof care is preventative maintenance.

notice that the hoof has two toes; each toe has a hard nail growing all along the outside edge and, to a lesser extent, along the inside between the toes. You'll know the nails are too long when the

outside nail has grown so much that it has started to curl underneath the toe, causing the sheep to walk on it. Any hoof that is cracked or delaminated should also be trimmed to prevent mud and poop from getting caked onto it.

Start by trimming this outside nail off until it's even with the pad and no longer curling underneath. Then continue around the front of the toe, making sure to cut the hard tip of the nail off so the toe becomes blunt rather than pointy. Next, cut back any of the inside nail that has also grown longer than the pad. I find that the outside edge and point tend to grow the most, with the inside edge growing very little and the back not at all. Finally, clean out between the two toes to make sure there isn't any mud or poop caked in there. There is a small scent gland located at the front of the hoof just where the two toes come together, which can become inflamed if it isn't kept clear. This gland would seem to be a major hazard to hoof health, given that sheep are walking in dirt and poop much of the time, but I have yet to see one plugged up on any of our sheep.

The key consideration when trimming hooves is to know when to stop. If you trim too much, you will cut into the living flesh of the pad and draw blood. This doesn't seem to hurt the sheep unduly, and most shepherds don't worry about a nick here or there. You can spray larger cuts with an antiseptic, such as Blue Cote, to help prevent any infection from setting in—which is a major risk of trimming hooves too aggressively. And if you trim the hooves too little? You'll just have to trim them more frequently. I was more than happy in the beginning to avoid drawing blood by trimming my sheeps' hooves frequently. Now that I have a better sense of where the nail ends and the pad begins, I'm a little more aggressive.

The final piece of preventative hoof care is making sure there aren't too many sharp obstacles that your sheep are likely to step on in their daily lives. Nails, sharp stones, or pointed stumps can all damage a sheep's hoof, especially if these hazards are in the barnyard where your sheep spend most of their time. Be sure to remove these obstacles. But don't worry about leveling every square inch of your pastures. Hooves aren't that fragile.

Once a summer or so, one of my sheep will turn up lame, and the question is why. In order of likelihood, here are the typical causes of lameness in sheep: untrimmed or poorly trimmed hooves, sprain or injury to the leg, stone or object caught between the toes, infected gland between the toes, too rich diet causing laminitis, or foot rot. If it's the hoof trimming or the lodged stone, you can quickly correct matters with your hoof trimmer. If it's the gland, laminitis, or foot rot, call the vet since antibiotics are likely to be required.

WORMS

Worms bedevil all of the earth's ungulates, including sheep. They live in an animal's digestive tract, where they lay eggs that are pooped out onto the ground. On the ground, the eggs hatch, and the next generation of worms climbs back up the grass stems to be eaten and returned to the friendly confines of the ovine gut. Wild ungulates, which roam over large areas, have it best when it comes to

 Above: A Suffolk lamb flock grazes near the edge of the woods at Harlow Brook Farm. The sheep are on one of the farm's three pastures, giving the other two pastures time to rest.

intestinal worms: by the time the new crop of worms has had the chance to climb up a nearby stem of grass to await being eaten, the deer or moose or antelope have moved on to greener (and hopefully worm-free) pastures. Our domesticated sheep, on the other hand, are either still in the affected pasture when the worms make their climb or are likely to return to that pasture within a few weeks. As a result, intestinal worms can go from being a minor nuisance that most sheep can tolerate to being a major problem that can lead to discomfort, malnutrition, and potentially death.

Your first line of defense against worms should be to rotate your pastures and, ideally, allow some of your pastures to rest from time to time to let the worm pressure die back. When my sheep move to their summer quarters, under their shade roof in the middle of our pasture, I can give the winter pastures near the barn three months off without grazing. If you have enough land to do something like this, so much the better.

It takes about three weeks for worms to go from being eggs freshly pooped out of the sheep to being larvae climbing up the grass, ready to be eaten. If the weather is wet during this period, the worm crop will be particularly large. If it's dry, fewer worms will hatch and live. If possible, try to time your pasture rotation so there are six or eight weeks between ovine visits to make sure you're avoiding the peak worm pressure at three to four weeks, especially when it's been wet.

Frost will knock back the worm population on your pastures, and winter will kill nearly all of them. In addition, the worm life cycle requires grassy pastures; worms won't hatch and infect your sheep if the eggs are deposited inside the shelter or on the hard-packed ground of the barnyard. All of which brings up the key question: in the winter, if the worms on the pasture are killed and the worms inside the shelter don't survive, where do next year's worms come from? The answer is called *hypobiosis*, a process in which worms spend the winter inside the sheep's gut by becoming dormant and surrounding themselves in protective cysts that resist the animal's attempts to digest them or force them out. Come spring, when fresh grass in the gut signals a favorable habitat outside, the worms return to life, emerge from the cysts, and start laying eggs for the next generation.

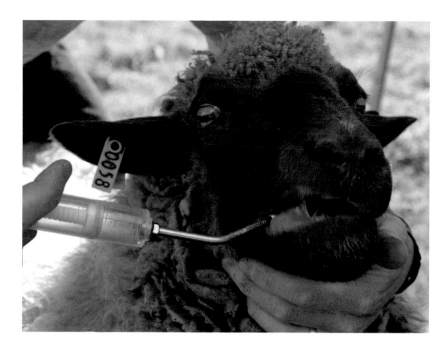

How will you know if your sheep are suffering from overexposure to worms? In a bad case, your sheep will start to lose weight and be lethargic despite being on good pasture. They may also have diarrhea, especially later in the summer when you know the diarrhea is not a function of going on pasture too quickly in the spring. Or, if your sheep are like mine, they will tell you when there's trouble. If I put my flock on nice, fresh pasture yet they baa and complain as if the pasture were dry and bare, I can be pretty sure they are suffering from too many intestinal worms.

 Above: The author demonstrates the use of a de-worming drench on Nina, a four-year-old Navajo-Churro ewe.

How to De-Worm Your Sheep

The simple solution to the problem of intestinal worms is to treat your sheep with a chemical de-wormer. There are two ways to do this: orally or via injection. Either way, the chemical kills the vast majority of the worms, and the sheep excrete the eggs and dead worms over the next twenty-four hours. After twenty-four hours have passed, you move your sheep to fresh, clean pasture, and you start again with a relatively clean slate.

Of the two methods, the oral route is the easier way to go. Step one is to contain the sheep in their confinement pen so you can easily administer the drench without having to chase them around. (Any liquid medication you administer orally to your sheep is called a *drench*.) Back a sheep into a corner of the pen (so that it can't get away from you), hold its head with one hand under its jaw, elevate its nose slightly so that the nostrils are about level with the eyes, tuck the tip of the drenching syringe into the corner of its mouth, and administer the de-wormer. (Consult the bottle to determine the proper dose.) Empty the syringe slowly enough so the sheep can keep up with you as you squeeze the liquid or paste into its mouth—but don't go so slowly that the sheep is being held longer than is necessary.

My sheep give me about a six-second window before they start to struggle in earnest. The key step is to elevate the nose slightly so the liquid doesn't spill out on the ground, but not so high that the liquid ends up running into the sheep's lungs. If your sheep cough after they've been drenched, liquid made it into the lungs. Just as in humans, small quantities of this are annoying but not fatal; larger quantities can lead to pneumonia and other complications. If you raise the nose no higher than the eyes, you should be fine. I know I've hit the sweet spot when the animal attempts to chew on the drenching syringe as I administer the dose; perhaps the presence of liquid in the esophagus triggers this reaction.

Injecting the De-Wormer

Injecting de-wormer is more complicated than drenching and also carries the slight risk of infection, because the skin is being punctured by a needle. Nevertheless, it isn't hard to inject a sheep once you get the hang of it. De-wormers are injected subcutaneously, meaning just under the skin and not into muscle. The technique is to find a loose flap of skin and pinch it between your thumb and index finger to create a tent. Given the long wool on sheep, finding loose skin can be much easier said than done; I find that the top of the front shoulder or the chest wall just behind the front armpit are both good spots. Once you have the tent, insert the needle so the tip is pushed into the middle of the tent, but not so far that it comes out the far side; then inject the liquid over the course of about two seconds or so.

For those of you unaccustomed to giving shots, and this included me a few years back, there are a few tricks to know when wielding a needle. First, make sure the liquid is at body temperature before injecting it; your sheep will appreciate this tremendously! Second, use a fresh needle for each injection. Using a needle multiple times makes it duller each time and introduces potential contamination back into the vial of medicine. Third, inject air into the vial equal to the volume of liquid you're about to withdraw; otherwise, you'll be slowly creating a vacuum in the vial that will make it impossible to withdraw future doses. And finally, fill your syringe with slightly more liquid than what you need for the dose, then withdraw the needle, hold the syringe vertically, tap any air bubbles up to the top, and expel the air bubbles from the syringe as you empty the syringe down to the correct dose. This prevents you from injecting air into the sheep.

For a subcutaneous injection, use a twenty-gauge needle that is one-half inch long. This is the best combination for reaching the middle of the tent without popping out the far side. If you see or feel any liquid seeping out onto the wool, you'll know you've overshot and need to try again. Needles are sold either separately from the syringe or integrated as one unit. I usually keep both types on hand and use the integrated unit if I'm treating just one animal; I use the removable syringe if I'm doing the whole flock and can take advantage of refilling the syringe.

Needless to say, having a second pair of hands available is very helpful when administering an injection. Your partner can hold the animal while you concentrate on the details of the shot. If you've never injected anything before, I'd recommend that you have a pro with you the first time. It's not particularly difficult, but I was quite nervous about it for the first few times.

The four most common classes of de-wormers on the market right now are sold under the trade names Lavamisole, Panacur, Ivermectin, and TBZ. Some or all of these de-wormers are available from your local veterinarian or online via one of the resources listed in the appendix. Prolonged use of the same de-wormer, year after year, can have the unintended effect of breeding a resistant strain of worm on your farm. For this reason, you should either rotate among several de-wormers throughout the year or switch to a different class every few years. And always use the full dose as printed on the label; using a partial dose, perhaps in the belief that your sheep are only lightly infected, will greatly speed up the development of resistant worms because you will only be killing the most susceptible worms and allowing the most resistant to live for another day.

When to De-Worm

There are four times for sure when you'll want to de-worm your sheep: two to four weeks before lambing, two to four weeks after lambing, at weaning, and just before winter. Why these times? Hormonal changes in a ewe associated with lambing help trigger the end of hypobiosis and the beginning of worm pressure in the spring; you want to insure that your ewes aren't losing any energy to worms just when they need all the energy they can get. Changes in the rumen associated with fresh pasture also trigger the growth of a new worm crop, so weaning is a convenient time to knock the worms back. Finally, de-worming just before winter, after all the worms in the environment have been killed by cold, insures that your flock will be worm-free for the winter.

These have been the only times I've had to de-worm my sheep in dry years, but I have enough pasture that I am able to rest an area for several months after it has been grazed several times. In wet years, I've had to de-worm several more times during the summer. By and large, I let the sheep tell me when they need de-worming: if I rotate them onto fresh, lush pasture but they still complain as if they were hungry, I know it's time for a round of de-wormer. I let them stay on this fresh pasture and move them to a new pasture twenty-four hours after de-worming them. This gives them a chance to poop out the worms and carcasses before moving to fresh grass.

Some shepherds, especially those who rotate their sheep across each pasture many times per summer, prefer to de-worm their sheep on a fixed schedule rather than wondering when the time is right. Every three weeks is the maximum amount of de-worming required, since it takes three weeks for a worm to grow from egg to larva. Shepherds facing heavy worm pressure will simply write the appropriate dates on the calendar and grab the drench when the appointed date arrives. Others will settle for the first of the month, or whenever it's time to start a new rotation across the pastures—or, like me, when they think their sheep are asking for it. The danger of de-worming too frequently is that you are wasting money on expensive de-wormer and speeding up the rate at which your particular worms become resistant to your particular de-wormer. The danger of de-worming not enough is that your sheep will not be as healthy as they should be, nor will the lambs grow as quickly as they might.

VACCINATIONS AND THE CD/T VACCINE

In addition to feed, hooves, and worms, the fourth major healthcare issue you should address with your sheep is the annual CD/T vaccine. CD/T stands for clostridium type C, clostridium type D, and tetanus; the first two prevent overeating problems in sheep, and the third, just as in humans, prevents infection from cuts and wounds. CD/T is a subcutaneous injection, so inject it just as you would inject a de-wormer.

If you go beyond CD/T and de-wormer in your life as a shepherd, it's worth knowing that some injections are intramuscular, as opposed to subcutaneous, which means that the needle goes straight into the flesh. Use a one-inch long, eighteen-gauge needle for this, which is longer than those used subcutaneously. The best place to give an intramuscular injection is the ropy muscle on the top of the shoulder, in front of the scapula. You don't want to inject a sheep just anywhere—both because you want to hit muscle and not an organ, and because an injection can cause an abscess in the muscle that will spoil the meat. Hold the sheep still, find the good muscles on the top of the shoulder, part the wool with your fingers so that you can see the skin, insert the needle all the way, and inject the dose over the course of about a second. As with a subcutaneous injection, make sure the liquid is at body temperature.

Above: The author prepares Nina for a vaccination on the shoulder.

You should never inject more than two ccs of liquid into any one spot on a sheep. If the dose calls for more than this, simply insert two ccs, remove the needle, and find another spot for the next (or remaining) part of the dose. A *cc* and an *ml* are interchangeable, so if the bottle prescribes a dosage in cc but your syringe is in ml, don't worry: one is the same as the other. Finally, note that nearly every vaccine or medication that you give to your sheep has a specific withdrawal time printed on the label, meaning that you should not slaughter an animal for food until the withdrawal time has passed.

EVERYTHING ELSE

There is a whole universe of maladies that can infect sheep, including many diseases that we share with our mammalian cousins such as polio, salmonella, and pneumonia. I don't think it's helpful for the beginning shepherd to focus too intently on all these potential catastrophes. As in rock climbing, you want to look up at where you're going, not down to where you hope to avoid. If you focus on the four areas just covered—feed, hooves, worms, and the CD/T vaccine—you'll have the big picture well in hand. Meanwhile, your vet is waiting for you at the bottom of the cliff should you peel off the rock unexpectedly.

How will you know if you're about to peel off? Once again, any sheep that is listless, not eating, refuses to get up, or is acting strangely should prompt a call to the vet if it doesn't straighten itself out in a few hours. A bout of diarrhea that lasts more than a few days is also reason to call.

Because proper diet is so important to the health of sheep, diarrhea is a good indication that all is not well. The most common causes of diarrhea in sheep are a rapid change in diet, too much rich feed (especially for young lambs), or too many worms. Once you've corrected the underlying problem, try giving the animal a day or two of Pepto-Bismol. Follow the directions printed for humans (sheep weigh about what we do). If this doesn't do the trick, call the vet.

A WORD ABOUT SCRAPIE

Scrapie is the ovine version of "mad cow" disease—a member of the spongiform encephalopathy family that includes chronic-wasting disease in deer and Creutzfeldt-Jakob disease in humans. Though scrapie is rare in sheep and extremely unlikely to turn up in a small-time flock, many states now have voluntary programs in place for monitoring and preventing the disease. If you are so inclined, I would encourage you to look into your state's program and consider enrolling your flock. I have not done so myself, because finding stud rams that are both certified purebred and certified scrapie-free has been too difficult locally. But I expect this will get easier over time, especially for flocks that are not registered purebreds.

CHAPTER TEN

Slaughter and Butchering

There is no point trying to sugarcoat it: killing animals is an intense and disturbing business. This is doubly true when the animals in question are ones you've fed and housed and raised from birth. All year long you've nurtured and cared for an animal and done your best to make it happy and healthy. Then you wake up one morning, pick up the proverbial knife, and do it in.

I was a vegetarian for five years during my early twenties, not because I was opposed to killing animals or eating meat, but because I didn't want to support the way animals were being treated in our industrial economy. I vowed that, should I ever leave the city and move to the country, I would try my hand at procuring my own meat.

Well, I did move. And before long, my wife and I were living on an old farm in the hills of Vermont. Whoops! What to do now? What was that vow I made—back in the safety of the city, far from the blood and guts and manure of the countryside—about procuring my own meat?

My first attempt was deer hunting. There are deer everywhere on our farm, and it seemed far more efficient to borrow a rifle from a friend than to put up fencing and get into the livestock business. But I only shot two deer in my first four years of trying—I didn't put much meat on our table. I quickly came to the same realization that our ancestors must have had more than 10,000 years ago: there's got to be a better way.

Opposite: A Suffolk lamb grazes on a mix of clover and Kentucky bluegrass in the pasture at Harlow Brook Farm. Owner Sarah Taylor and her husband keep about a dozen sheep each summer for fall butchering. "It's pretty cheap food," she said.

Shooting deer helped prepare me for having blood on my hands—not the indirect, metaphorical blood of animals killed on my behalf far away, but the warm, red kind. I immediately understood why hunting cultures develop elaborate rituals for both attracting and then thanking their prey; deer are so wary and rarely seen at close range that you can't help but think the animal you've killed has "offered" itself to you in some way.

Slaughtering livestock is a whole different story. There's no luck, no element of chance, no illusion of a life freely offered. You've raised these animals from birth, and while they have slowly placed their trust in you, it turns out you've been planning to kill them all along. The expression "Lambs to the slaughter" conveys such horror because of the implied deception—not just because of the certain death, but because naiveté and trust go under the knife with the lamb. They don't with the fawn.

How do you prepare yourself for this? The rituals developed by hunting cultures actually served two purposes: the obvious one of thanking and honoring the animal for giving you its life, and the subtler one of preparing the hunter to become a killer. I'd never thought about the second part until I became a killer myself.

Which brings me to my main point: because you and I live in a relatively non-land-based culture where few people are involved with killing animals, you are very likely to find yourself slaughtering your sheep some evening after getting home from your day job or doing the deed some weekend afternoon before meeting up with friends for dinner and a movie. There'll be no elaborate dance of celebration the night before, no drumming, no fires—and none of the camaraderie of living in hunting camp for a week. You're apt to be making small talk with your friends over a can of beer only an hour after experiencing some of the most intense moments of your life.

I'm not suggesting that you invent rituals or study shamanism to prepare yourself for slaughter day. I am, however, suggesting that at the very least you take a few deep breaths, see if you can clear your calendar a bit, and recognize that mental preparation is far and away the most difficult part of slaughter day.

OPTIONS FOR SLAUGHTER DAY

In comparison, the actual logistics of slaughter day are straightforward. In preparing for the day, you can choose one of the following options, listed in increasing order of intensity and effort.

1. Have your animals picked up and taken to a slaughterhouse.

 Above: Tom Eaton skins a Navajo-Churro ram lamb during butchering at a barn in Vermont. Eaton does farm slaughtering as a sideline to his main job working as a landscaper.

Above: The author puts wooden sides on his pickup truck before transporting his sheep.

2. Drive your animals to the slaughterhouse yourself.
3. Hire someone to come to your place, slaughter the animals, and then take the carcasses to a butcher shop for cutting.
4. Do it all yourself.

Each method, as usual, has distinct advantages and disadvantages.

HAVE THEM PICKED UP

This method requires only a simple telephone call to arrange for the pickup and has the additional advantage that you can "blame" the driver for taking your sheep away and killing them. But if your goal with raising sheep was to get involved and take responsibility for the meat you eat, you're essentially abdicating at the crucial moment by averting your eyes.

DRIVE THEM YOURSELF

Driving your sheep yourself keeps you involved in the process and prevents you from pretending that it isn't happening. In addition, it gives you the chance to take a peek inside the slaughterhouse door, which, if you're like me, you'll want to do at least once before slaughter day to make sure that the killing happens in a quick and painless way.

Anyone who claims that sheep are dumb animals that don't know killing when they see it is simply not paying attention. I've had to hold sheep down on the ground to give them vaccines, trim their hooves, and prepare them to be shot for slaughter. If the sheep know that it's the latter, there's no mistaking their terror for the mere indignation they display when it's the former. At the end of one particularly bad episode, when I held down the last lamb from a group that had been able to watch the whole slaughter going on, I could scarcely hold on to her because her heart was beating so fast.

Take a look inside the slaughterhouse and talk to the people who work there. If the moment of slaughter takes place in a quick and efficient way, out of sight of other animals, then you've found your place. If not, keep looking.

Getting the lambs from your place to the slaughterhouse can be a challenge in and of itself. My preferred method is to take our pickup truck and put tall wooden sides on the back and rear to make a pen that is too deep for the sheep to see or jump over (roughly three and a half feet tall). I back the truck into the barn right next to the pen, and then two of us load each lamb while a third person minds the tailgate to see that lambs go into the truck but not back out. The advantage of doing all this in the barn is

that the lambs are still contained should one escape from our grasp during the loading.

An alternative method is to back the truck into the barnyard and carry the lambs from the confinement pen to the truck using the barnyard fence as your safety net. A horse trailer or smaller trailer specifically designed for sheep is even better since you don't have to

 Above: A flock of Katahdins runs across the pasture during a sheep dog trial. Flock-owner Allan Lynch raises the breed for meat because of their mild taste and ease of butchering. Katahdins have fur instead of wool.

Above: Tom Eaton shoots a ram lamb. Eaton and a co-worker skin and gut the animals on the farm before they're taken off-site for packaging the meat into cuts.

lift the lambs far off the ground to get them inside. If you or someone in your neighborhood has such a trailer, fabulous. If not, you'll have to round up some friends and heft the lambs into a pickup truck, as I do. A pickup truck with a cap on the bed works well, too, if you don't have tall sides.

HIRE SOMEONE TO COME TO YOUR PLACE

For a variety of financial and legal reasons, there are far fewer slaughterhouses these days than there used to be—despite that fact that we eat more meat than ever. You may therefore decide that it is more convenient to hire someone to come to your farm than to take your animals elsewhere. This will save you the trouble of driving your sheep someplace else, which your sheep will surely appreciate, and also give you some control over how the slaughter takes place.

Before the big day, figure out the logistics of how your sheep will go from the pen where you are holding them to the place where they will be killed. This is crucial: you'll want to move them far enough away so as not to disturb the others but close enough that you won't have to manhandle them too hard to get them there. Even if a sheep doesn't know why it is being singled out from the flock, it is still going to resist your efforts and try to get away. The last thing you want on slaughter day is a jailbreak or mass escape, which will be unnecessarily traumatic for both you and the sheep. Make sure that your pens and fencing are up to the task and not just jury-rigged for the moment.

Once an animal has been killed, your thoughts need to turn immediately to ensuring that the meat is of the highest quality possible. The person you hire to do the slaughter will tell you what is needed, but the general scene usually looks like this: the animal is killed with a single shot from a .22 caliber rifle at the base of the skull, the carotid artery is immediately slit open to allow as much blood to escape the body as possible, and the carcass is then gutted, skinned, relieved of hooves and head, and hung up to cool. The less time that elapses between the moment of death and the moment when the carcass is fully cooled, the better the meat will be.

Clearly, you'll need to do all this in a place that can get a little messy. Letting the blood soak into the ground is the easiest approach, though you could also spread a bunch of sawdust to soak it up. (If you're planning to save the pelt, however, the sawdust will get lodged into the wool and make life difficult later on.) You'll also need a way to dispose of the guts, hooves, and heads. Ideally, and for a fee, the butcher will take these away for disposal later on.

If not, you'll need to do this job yourself—and the sooner, the better. Guts smell quite sweet and pleasant when they first come tumbling out of

the carcass, but they quickly become putrid upon exposure to air. I usually wrap the skins and heads in trash bags and take them to the landfill, since they will not readily decompose. Then I spread the rest on the ground in a far corner of our farm, far enough away so the coyotes won't associate this free buffet with the sheep still living in the paddocks. Or I bury it under the compost pile if I happen to have a good pile going.

Though the person you've hired might butcher the animals right on your farm, it's far more likely that he or she will take the carcasses back to a cutting shop and work on them once the meat has cooled. Unlike beef, the flavor of lamb and mutton does not necessarily improve with age, so the carcasses do not need to hang any longer than is necessary for full cooling. Upon butchering, the meat should either be eaten, refrigerated, or frozen right away.

Do It Yourself

The ultimate pinnacle in taking responsibility for your own meat production, and one that I have yet to attain, is to both slaughter and butcher your sheep yourself. You can hire or borrow friends to help, of course, but you get to be involved at every step of the way.

Besides the ethical purity of the do-it-yourself approach, there's the advantage of having complete control over how your animals are handled and how your meat is prepared. I would strongly discourage the new shepherd from attempting this approach for the simple reason that there's an awful lot to know before you start slaughtering animals on your own; if things don't go as planned, it will be very easy for you to inadvertently, well, butcher the job. If you have experience as a butcher or know someone who does, great. Otherwise, choose one of the other options on the list for your first few times. There's no shame in letting a skilled expert do it right, especially when you consider the pain and stress you'll be inflicting on your sheep as a bumbling beginner.

Opposite: Nineteen-year-old Clint Hill skins a ram lamb. He has been working as a butcher for about two years. Hill follows in the footsteps of his grandfather and father, who are butchers. "I'll probably end up doing it forever," he said.

CUTS OF MEAT

Before slaughter day, you should put some thought into how you want your meat to show up at the freezer door. Do you prefer roasts, chops, burger, or stew meat? The choice is yours, and you have choices to make.

In general, you can have all of the meat on your sheep ground up for burger or cut into stew meat if you so desire. Any butchered sheep that is older than about fourteen months is considered to be mutton, not lamb. Mutton will have a flavor whose strength and sheep-like taste will have increased as the animal grew older: the older the sheep, the stronger the taste. Though many people prefer the strong taste of mutton chops and roasts, most Americans do not—and hence most mutton in this country is butchered into burger or stew meat. Not only does this make it easy to prepare soups, stews, or sausages; it also removes the meat from the bones so that additional strength of flavor isn't imparted to the meat after packaging.

If you have a lamb, however, or if you love mutton, you should certainly consider limiting the amount of burger or stew meat to those parts of the animal that don't otherwise make good chops or roasts. Here is an overview of the most common ways in which a lamb can be butchered. If you have, at the very least, a sense of the big picture before you speak with your butcher, you'll be much better informed than I was my first year:

"How do you want your lambs cut?" the butcher asked.

"I don't know....How about a normal cut," I said.

"A normal cut?" he said, his eyes filled with pleading, loathing, scorn, and despair. "You want a normal cut?"

Oops—lesson learned. There's no such thing as a "normal cut" in the lamb world. If I hadn't been wearing my Red Sox cap, I think he might have booted me out right then and there. As it was, I ended up switching butchers two years later, once I realized that I couldn't look him in the eye without forever remembering my initial gaffe.

- **Legs.** With a lamb, the rear legs are the marquee cuts and the first things you should think about, because roast leg of lamb is one of the very most wonderful

Right: Marian White has some of her lamb meat packaged into maple sausage at a federally inspected facility.

meat dishes in the whole wide world. You can keep both rear legs whole, or you can have one or both of them *butterflied*—whereby the meat is cut back and the leg bone is removed. This makes for a sumptuous meal on the grill. On a large lamb you can also have a steak or two cut off of the top of the leg in order to keep the leg down to a manageable size.

- **Chops.** Chops are probably the second most popular cut of lamb after the leg, and they can be left together (as a rack of lamb) or cut singly (one rib per chop, or a double thickness of two ribs per chop). Individual chops are usually made with the loin vertebrae, either single- or double-thickness.

- **Shoulder.** The shoulder can either be left whole, boned, cut up for stew meat, or ground into burger. The shoulder meat tends to be fattier than the legs and chops, so it is usually better suited to the oven or stew pot than the grill. The first year, try leaving one shoulder whole for roasting and have the other cut up for stewing, just so you get a sense of the variety.

- **Shanks.** The shanks are the remainder of the front legs, below the shoulder, and though they are often deboned for burger or stew meat, they can also be kept intact for braising or soup.

- **Ribs.** The ribs can also be kept together for grilling and barbeque, though there isn't much meat on lamb ribs and most people have the meat removed for stew and burger.

- **Organs.** To some, the meat from the heart, liver, kidneys, and tongue is divine. To others, the organs are too gross to ponder. You should let your butcher know which side of this fence you sit on. I find myself more on the latter side, but our dog is enthusiastically on the former.

- **The rest.** Have everything else, which includes the meat on the neck and the ends of the legs either cut up for stew meat or ground into burger, depending on your preference. Or, consider having it mixed with herbs and spices and ground into sausage.

How much meat will a typical lamb yield? Volume-wise, about two brown shopping bags full. (Make sure you have space in your freezer or chest freezer for the meat once you pick it up from the butcher.) In general, a lamb with a live weight of 100 pounds will have a hanging weight (head, hooves, skin, and innards removed) of roughly 60 pounds and a final, butchered weight of 40 to 50 pounds.

PAPER OR PLASTIC?

Your last decision is whether to have your meat wrapped in butcher paper or in the Styrofoam-tray-with-plastic-wrap-covering that is becoming increasingly common for all meats these days. The advantage of paper is that it is usually the simplest and cheapest way to go; the disadvantage is that blood can leak through the paper if the meat isn't frozen immediately after being wrapped. Styrofoam solves the blood problem neatly yet creates excessive packaging waste and doesn't, in my view, resist freezer burn nearly as well as properly wrapped butcher paper. A third option is Cryovac packaging, which is sort of like shrink-wrapping in thicker plastic with all the air removed. This solves the aforementioned problems yet is often more expensive than either of the other two methods. Not all butchers can do Cryovac packaging. If yours can, it's often worth the expense—except when you are sure you'll be eating all of the meat within a month or two of it being frozen.

KEEPING MEAT TENDER

Various books talk about the *Tenderstretch method* of hanging sheep carcasses to insure that the meat, especially from the rear legs and loins, is as tender as possible. Traditionally, meat animals are hung in the butcher's cooler by their Achilles' tendons; but in the Tenderstretch method, a sheep is hung by its Aitch bone (part of the pelvis) instead of by the Achilles. The advantage is said to be that the rear legs can hang in a more normal position, which keeps the leg and loin muscles relaxed and long.

The problem I've had is that none of the butchers I've worked with have ever heard of this method and don't seem much interested in finding out.

Plus, the meat we've eaten (hung the usual way) has been very tender indeed. I guess I'll keep asking around to see if Tenderstretch is starting to catch on; but if you ask your butcher about it and get the blank stare in return, don't worry. If you've raised happy and healthy animals with free access to grass and the outdoors, the meat is going to be mighty tasty regardless of how the carcass was oriented in the cooler.

SHEEPSKINS

Unless you instruct otherwise, your butcher will dispose of all the leftover parts of your sheep for you. This includes the head, feet, innards, and skin. Though you'd have to be a serious scrounger to find use for the first three items on this list, sheepskins are another story.

If you would like to save a skin or two to turn into a sheepskin rug or chair covering, you should let the butcher know in advance. Sheepskins that are being prepared for tanning are "pulled" from the carcass rather than cut, which works exactly the way it sounds. A stray knife slice will make a skin impossible to commercially tan as the cut will tear apart in the machinery. A pulled skin, on the other hand, will look great and hold together well. But it places more demands on the butcher, who will use a knife unless otherwise directed.

As soon as the skin is pulled from the carcass, it should be rubbed (on the flesh side) with a thick layer of salt to draw out the water and prevent the skin from becoming brittle, cracking, or molding. If your butcher will do this, so much the better. If not, you'll need to arrange to bring some salt with you (use coarse livestock salt, not expensive table salt) and be on hand during the skinning. Figure on having three to five pounds of salt per pelt—using three for a small lamb and up to five for a mature ewe or ram. Keep the skin well covered in salt for at least two weeks before scraping it clean and sending the skin to a commercial tanning house for processing. Or, if you're truly dedicated and one of the serious scroungers I mentioned earlier, you can learn how to tan the skin yourself. Just make sure you saved the sheep's brains during the butchering!

Opposite: The sheepskin of Molé, a Navajo-Churro lamb, is displayed on a gate at Sunrise Farm.

MARKETING, LEGALITIES, AND THE FINE PRINT

Selling lamb and mutton is not as easy as filling up a chest freezer and then roping in passersby on the street. The federal and many state governments have a say in the process, and while their say helps protect the national meat supply from all kinds of nasty stuff, it also makes life quite difficult for the small-time shepherd. It's easy to meet the letter of the law if you're a big packing company that can hire full-time meat inspectors; it's quite the opposite when you're talking a half-dozen lambs once per year.

The tried-and-true approach of many a small-time shepherd is to pre-sell the lambs, alive, to whomever will be the ultimate customer. That's because animals that are slaughtered for their owner's personal use are exempt from U.S. Department of Agriculture (USDA) inspection. The law is primarily concerned with protecting unknowing customers from having unsafe meat foisted on them. If individuals, on the other hand, bring in their own animals for their own use, the USDA figures they are doing so with their eyes open.

Here's how this works logistically on your end. Your customer writes you a check to buy a specific animal, writes the butcher a check for the slaughter fee, and fills out a waiver (saying that this meat is for their own personal use and not for resale) for the butcher. Then you, since you are handling the logistics, have the animals slaughtered and arrange to deliver the wrapped meat to the customer, who is already the animal's owner.

Many rural butchers are small-timers who are not USDA certified, so this "whole animal" approach may be your only legal option for selling your meat. If your butcher is a USDA-certified facility, however, your options are broader. You can still sell your customers whole animals, but there's no waiver to fill out, and they write you one check for the meat when they pick it up. You can also sell them halves, quarters, or even individual cuts because the meat is USDA inspected. The downside, however, is that the USDA inspector needs to be paid too, so the slaughter fee is usually higher at USDA-approved facilities.

If you're thinking that the USDA will look the other way if you're only selling meat to your friends, think again. According to the law, noninspected meat can only be eaten by you, your immediate family, and your non-paying guests. I have had no trouble convincing my customers that they should buy the whole lamb, so don't mess around and take the chance of getting caught selling individual cuts. Plus, if you were in the business of selling lamb by the cut instead of by the animal, you personally would be eating a lot of lamb shoulder in your life and would never taste a leg or chop again.

FINAL THOUGHTS ON THE DEATH OF ANIMALS

I have covered the major logistics and concerns to keep in mind when slaughtering lambs and sheep. There are emotional matters too. You may find yourself adrift in a sea of emotions as the big day approaches. I know I do. I feel embarrassed and ashamed, especially in front of our ewes, when I drag their lambs off to be killed. I feel some amount of revulsion when the knife cuts the throat, though I confess that this has lessened over time as it's become more familiar. And I feel pride and excitement when the meat is all wrapped and ready for my grill or my friends' freezers.

I used to have a simple if-it-looks-bad-it-is-bad understanding of how things worked in the natural world. I miss the marvelous simplicity of those days! There are many aspects of slaughtering your own animals that look very bad indeed; be prepared for hard questions and harder looks from friends and acquaintances whose primary knowledge of nature comes from watching Bambi at the movies. But living with sheep and eating their meat is among the most profound and meaningful things I do in life. I'd be surprised if you don't end up feeling the same way, too.

CHAPTER ELEVEN

Some Final Thoughts

With the nitty-gritty details out of the way, I want to address three last topics that don't otherwise fit into any one of the previous chapters: raising sheep organically, handling sheep, and living with both sheep and children.

A WORD ABOUT ORGANIC

My main job in life these days is growing organic vegetables, so I'm quite familiar with the rules and regulations behind certified-organic agriculture. Plus, I'm a firm believer in the benefits of organic agriculture in general: for the farmer, the consumer, and for the land. I naturally assumed, therefore, when I started raising sheep, that I would raise them organically. But that's not how it's turned out so far.

Not knowing anything about raising sheep, I took the booklet of organic regulations to my friend from whom I was buying the flock. "I want to raise my sheep organically," I said. "Would you look at this and tell me what you think?"

He thumbed through page after page, and as the minutes started to drag on, I could tell that this wasn't going exactly the way I had hoped. Finally he turned to me and gave me what I now know to be extremely good advice: "If you want to do this at some point in the future, I think you'll be able to pull it off. But I wouldn't do this starting out—that's for sure!"

There are two difficulties with raising your sheep organically, in my opinion. The first is that *organic* in the animal world often comes at the expense of *local*, which is something I also feel strongly about. My neighboring farmer's hay, although rich and wonderful and harvested from fields that have been well cared for by his family for more than a century, is not certified organic. Similarly, the grain sold by my local feed store, while produced by a local company, is not certified organic. If and when I decide to raise my sheep organically, therefore, I will be doing so at the expense of my neighborhood farming economy, which I am reluctant to do.

The second—and more formidable—problem with raising animals organically is the question of what to do when they get sick. Most animals get sick from time to time, including usually healthy human animals such as myself. But while I can take advantage of modern medicine to cure myself, I can't do so to cure my sheep. That's a bit of an oversimplification, but not much. The general point is that medications that we ourselves typically use—and freely use on our pet dogs and cats—cannot be used on certified organic sheep. Your best option when a certified animal gets sick is to treat it and move it into a second flock that you are raising non-organically side by side with the organic flock. And if you're a small-time shepherd such as myself, running two mini-flocks creates logistical and financial problems that are not trivial.

Don't get me wrong: I'm an ardent supporter of organic agriculture and a firm believer in keeping animals healthy, rather than treating them when they get sick. I plan to convert my flock to organic status in the next few years, or at least try to. It's just that I think the organic regulations are too restrictive for anyone just starting out who is not ready or willing to run two herds side by side. So I'll give you the same advice my friend gave to me at the outset of my shepherding career: keep organic in mind for the future, but don't start out that way.

Instead, I keep three core principals of organic shepherding in mind at all times: free-range, grass-fed, and minimally medicated. My flock can wander inside and outside 99.99% of the time, with that remaining .01% coming on the few nights during lambing season when I close the door to make sure an expecting ewe doesn't give birth out on the back 40 somewhere. The percentage of food that my sheep get from grass is harder to calculate, but I feed them grain only during flushing and pre-lambing, because grass-fed animals are both healthier in life and provide healthier meat for our table. Finally, whenever an animal requires medical attention, I do my very best not only to treat the symptoms but also to figure out how to prevent the situation from recurring in the future.

If you follow these three guidelines as best you can, you're going to raise some very happy sheep indeed. Whether or not they are organically certified is something you can address later once you become an old hand.

HOW TO HANDLE YOUR SHEEP

Handling your sheep properly helps keep them happy and healthy. The reverse is also true: both shepherd and sheep can be injured or mightily distressed by mishandling. Here are a few overall tips to make life easier for you and your sheep.

First, try to go to your sheep instead of bringing them to you. When it's time for me to give my

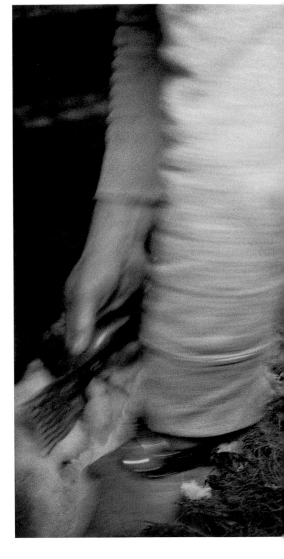

sheep a de-wormer, for example, or even if I want to examine just one sheep, I wait until they are already lying down in the shelter rather than rounding them up out on a pasture somewhere. Then I simply walk over, close the gate, and press them into their confinement pen. I'm not huffing and puffing, they're not upset at having been worked too hard, and there's

no chance of an animal getting up a good head of steam and making a break for it.

Rams, especially, will make a run at you if they think there's a chance of escape. When pressing rams into the confinement

Above: Clover is sheared while sitting on her butt at Sunrise Farm. Sheep become docile and immobile in a sitting position.

 Above: Tommy Woodbury, age seven, tries to hug a Border Leicester/ Romney ewe at the Tunbridge World's Fair in Vermont. Woodbury was visiting with his school class, an annual tradition for kids on the first day of the fair.

pen, be sure to keep your fingers entirely on your side of whatever gate or panel you're using to close them in. The second year we had a ram on our place, he made a run at me and crushed my thumb between his horns and the metal gate I was holding. It took more than a year for my thumb to fully recover, and looking back on the scene as it unfolded, I'm quite sure that he aimed for my hands once he saw that I wasn't keeping my fingers on my side of the gate.

Second, the key to controlling a sheep is to keep its head up. With a ram that has horns, it's relatively straightforward: grab him by the handles and lift. Two people can walk a ram around quite successfully by lifting him by the horns until his front legs are off the ground. Then you can walk him forward, backward, or side to side. As long as his front legs remain off the ground, he's yours.

It's more complicated for a ewe (or a polled ram), but the idea is to slide your arm under her neck and reach around to either grab the back of her head or rest your hand on her back. Be prepared for the ewe to occasionally try to jerk her head back down—for she knows she's good and strong when her head is down but weak and vulnerable when it's up. Moving her backward is also a bit more of a project. If there are two of you, just lift her head high and push her backward, using your bodies to keep her from moving sideways. If there's just one of you, grab her by the stub of her tail with one hand while holding her head up with the other and walk backward. This sometimes works for me. If it doesn't, I'll let her work her way over to the wall of the shelter and then press her there with my body weight, lifting her head to move her backward.

Third, never grab a sheep by its wool. You can damage the wool and damage the skin underneath the wool that you've grabbed. Plus, unlike holding a sheep's head up, grabbing the wool doesn't cause the animal to relax and give up: it causes the animal to renew its efforts at escape. Even if you manage to keep hold of the sheep, you will have caused it to become very agitated and upset.

Fourth, if you're dealing with a lamb that is small enough to lift, just circle your arms right around the outside of all four legs, clasp your hands together on the far side, and lift. The lamb's head will hang over one arm and the butt over the other, and if the lamb kicks its legs to struggle, it'll have nothing to get a purchase on.

Fifth, as I mentioned in the health chapter, if you want to trim hooves or otherwise immobilize a sheep, the best thing to do is sit it on its butt and hold its head up. (Actually, sit it on its pelvis on one side of the tail, not straight on the tail itself—ouch!) This is easier said than done, so watch your shearer do

it the next time he or she stops by. The real pros can lean an animal against their legs and tuck the head back through their thighs to hold it in place. It's an amazing feat: the sheep usually gives up, relaxes, and sits there like a big pile of wool.

Sixth, always lead your sheep from in front and don't try to push them from behind. Use the grain trick to have them follow you around. Leading from in front will cause the flock to form a tight group as they each seek to get into the middle, close to you. Pushing from behind will have just the opposite effect as they peel off to get away from you.

Finally, as long as you're going to be living with sheep, you might as well learn to be polite about it. Though my parents always told me that making good eye contact was an important way to make friends and influence people, you will quickly discover that the opposite is true in ovine society. My sheep will hoof it to the far corner of the pen if I walk deliberately toward them, staring right into their eyes. (This is actually a good trick to remember when you're trying to stop them from sneaking through a gate that you left open by mistake.) But if I stroll into their pen looking down at my feet or gazing off to the side, quietly saying "Hi girls" or "Good morning ladies" as I approach, I can usually walk right up and scratch one of them behind the ears without creating any commotion at all.

CHILDREN AND SHEEP

Children and sheep go well together, for the obvious reason that having sheep around can teach children responsibility and empathy, all in relative safety. When it comes to livestock, sheep are about as easy and manageable as it gets; they aren't inherently aggressive, they don't tower over children and intimidate

 Above. Two boys pet sheep in their pen at a local fair. Fairs give kids a chance to see and interact with different breeds of farm animals.

them, and they won't kill or injure a child with a capricious kick or head butt. Children can go into the barn unattended and do the daily chores without risk to life and limb.

There are two exceptions to this genteel picture. First, I wouldn't let any child who isn't at least a head taller than the largest sheep go into their pen untended. Adult sheep weigh as much as many adult humans, and a child carrying food who doesn't command immediate respect could get accidentally jostled and injured in a feeding frenzy. If you have small children, therefore, make sure that food and water can be dispensed from outside the pen without having to open the gate and walk in.

Second, don't keep a ram if you have children; and if you do have a ram, don't let your children handle the ram chores unattended. A solid butting from a ram can be very painful and harmful, even for an adult. For a child, it could be fatal. Even the most mild-mannered ram will use his horns to determine his standing in the world, so your job as an adult is to make sure he doesn't have the opportunity to try that on your child.

Sheep are especially good with shy children, and vice versa. On numerous occasions, I've watched a pack of kids run into our barn, go up to the sheep pen, and stick their hands in to try to pet the sheep. The sheep, of course, recoil from such aggressive behavior and do their best to avoid all the outstretched hands. But sooner or later, I'll notice that some child—almost invariably a shy one—has somehow managed to start petting one of them. A sheep sidled up to the railing where no hands were poking through, the child eased a tentative hand out, and soon there was a happy sheep rubbing against eager fingers and a kid with a smile the size of the moon.

For more confident and assertive children, there's also good stuff to be learned here. Not everyone, human or animal alike, responds well to the direct approach. Some folks don't answer right away or won't open up until they've gotten to know you a bit. Living with sheep can teach a confident child the beauty of the sidelong glance, the indirect inquiry, the all-in-due-time attitude. Sheep are not malicious but are certainly skeptical—and they draw from a deep reservoir of patience. These are not bad qualities to teach a child.

You, the adult, can make it easier for your sheep and children to bond by arranging frequent opportunities to socialize. Move your flock into its confinement pen, bring in a few stools, and allow your children and sheep to get to know one another. Sheep love to be scratched on their necks, behind their ears, and on their backs; once your flock decides that you aren't about to harm them, your kids will discover that a line has formed of eager animals waiting to be scratched. Teach your children that sheep don't like to be patted on the head like the family dog. Butting heads is how sheep maintain their hierarchy, and patting one on the head is kind of like saying, "You wanna take this outside?" Which, of course, you don't.

IN CONCLUSION

Shortly after I graduated from college, I went to visit a friend on a dairy farm in southern Vermont. My first morning there, we woke well before dawn on a crisp winter night and walked across the barnyard under an unbroken roof of iridescent stars. Inside the barn, my friend flicked on the light, and soon we were swimming in a warm sea of Brown Swiss dairy cows, guiding animals to their stalls, spreading grain and hay for them to eat, and setting up the milking equipment.

My most vivid memory of that morning is of the cows' breath: large volumes of air moving in and out of warm lungs, smoothly and gently, waves lapping on a beach, an occasional wave breaking over my neck and face as a cow turned her head to see what I was up to. Their breath smelled like summer grass—a revelation, coming so quickly on the heels of crunching boots on snow. And the sound of them chewing away, lips snuffling hay and grain and setting it against teeth to start chewing, was like being in a room full of uncles and aunts all talking quietly and easily among themselves—a world of murmurs and conversation with no undercurrent, no rush, no plan to move on to bigger and better things.

We talk a lot in our society about New Age qualities: feeling connected, being soulful, living in the moment, and feeling rooted and grounded. Cows can't talk, of course, so they don't: they just are these creatures who personify the very values that seem so elusive and intangible in human affairs. I don't believe I had any idea of what "grounded" meant until that first morning when I walked among the dairy cows and listened to them breathe. But from that moment on, I was hooked.

Sheep are the same as cows: they are certainly smaller and shyer but struck from the same mold. I think all of the barnyard animals are soulful, to a greater or lesser extent— although the horse strikes me as too spirited and the goat too inquisitive to fully realize the type. When I crunch across our dooryard on a winter's morning, flick on the barn light, and offer up a pile of green hay to my eager and grateful girls, I'm right back in that ocean of contentment, an occasional warm, summery breath catching me in the face as I bend down toward the feeder.

Sheep are manageable. They're small, even-tempered, and generally eager to please. Watch their ears. Note the angle of their heads. They have a lot to say. Before you know it, you'll understand almost every word. And by then, you will have been taken in as an honorary member of the flock. A very soulful flock indeed.

Right: Bradford Jones, age four, and Emma Hansen, three, follow Spot the bottle lamb into the barn at Fat Rooster Farm. Bradford Jones' family has run the organic family farm for nearly eight years.

The Shepherd's Year

With all the various dates being mentioned in this book, I thought it would be helpful to assemble many of them together into one concise calendar.

November first is the key day in my shepherding year: it's roughly when the last grass hereabouts is irretrievably killed by frost (meaning that it's time for the lambs to go to slaughter), and it's an ideal date for the ram to be put in with the ewes in order for the lambs to be born in early April. I've gone ahead and put this calendar together based on that November first date. If you decide that a different date works better for your schedule and climate, go ahead and make any adjustments you need.

January

Feed
- Score ewes and adjust winter hay ration accordingly.

Management
- Call shearer and arrange for shearing in early March.

February

Feed
- Score ewes mid-month, increase hay ration, and start grain if needed for lamb growth.

March

Feed
- Score ewes to determine ideal grain amount to get them to 3+.

Management
- Buy lambing supplies, fix up creep and jugs.
- Shearing day.
- Clean out winter manure.

Healthcare
- Trim hooves; administer CD/T vaccine, de-wormer.

April

Feed
- Supply grain for ewes during lactation.

Management
- Lambs are born over a roughly three-week window.
- Dock lamb tails at twenty-four hours.
- Arrange to buy hay for next winter
- Set up creep for lambs.
- Check fences and make any needed repairs.

Healthcare
- Give first CD/T vaccine to all lambs by month's end and install ear tags.
- De-worm ewes after all lambs are born.

May

Feed
- Increase grain in creep for lambs.
- Slowly start ewes on pasture, an hour or so per day at first.
- Stop grain to ewes.

Healthcare
- Give second CD/T to lambs one month after first.

June

Feed

End grain for lambs and remove creep.

Management

- Find buyers, if you plan to sell breeding stock.
- Arrange for a ram to be around in the fall.
- Arrange slaughter date and details.

Healthcare

- De-worm flock if needed.
- Wean lambs.

July

Management

- Ram lambs need to be kept separate from ewes from now on.

Healthcare

- De-worm flock if needed.

August

Management

- Purchase hay and store it in the barn.
- Arrange for September shearing day, if desired.

Healthcare

- De-worm flock if needed.

September

Management

- Second shearing day, if desired.
- Finalize meat sales with buyers.

Healthcare

- Trim hooves.
- De-worm flock if needed.

October

Feed

- Score ewes, start flushing ewes with grain as needed.

November

Management

- Lambs go to slaughter.
- Ram with ewes for forty-five days, grain for all.

Healthcare

- Final de-worming before winter.

December

Feed

- Score ewes, and continue feeding grain until end of the month if needed.

Management

- Separate ram from ewes mid-month.

Ewe Gestation Table

Here's a handy reference guide for figuring out when your lambs will start being born, based on when you introduced the ram.

DATE BRED	DATE DUE	DATE BRED	DATE DUE
Jan. 1	May 29	Jun. 30	Nov. 25
Jan. 6	Jun. 3	Jul. 10	Dec. 5
Jan. 11	Jun. 8	Jul. 15	Dec. 10
Jan. 16	Jun. 13	Jul. 20	Dec. 15
Jan. 21	Jun. 18	Jul. 25	Dec. 20
Jan. 26	Jun. 23	Jul. 30	Dec. 25
Jan. 31	Jun. 28	Aug. 4	Dec. 30
Feb. 5	Jul. 3	Aug. 9	Jan. 4
Feb. 10	Jul. 8	Aug. 14	Jan. 9
Feb. 15	Jul. 13	Aug. 19	Jan. 14
Feb. 20	Jul. 18	Aug. 24	Jan. 19
Feb. 25	Jul. 23	Aug. 29	Jan. 24
Mar. 2	Jul. 28	Sep. 3	Jan. 29
Mar. 7	Aug. 2	Sep. 8	Feb. 3
Mar. 12	Aug. 7	Sep. 13	Feb. 8
Mar. 17	Aug. 12	Sep. 18	Feb. 13
Mar. 22	Aug. 17	Sep. 23	Feb. 18
Mar. 27	Aug. 22	Sep. 28	Feb. 23
Apr. 1	Aug. 27	Oct. 3	Feb. 28
Apr. 6	Sep. 1	Oct. 8	Mar. 5
Apr. 11	Sep. 6	Oct. 12	Mar. 10
Apr. 16	Sep. 11	Oct. 17	Mar. 15
Apr. 21	Sep. 16	Oct. 22	Mar. 20
Apr. 26	Sep. 21	Oct. 27	Mar. 25
May 1	Sep. 26	Nov. 2	Mar. 30
May 6	Oct. 1	Nov. 7	Apr. 4
May 11	Oct. 6	Nov. 12	Apr. 9
May 16	Oct. 11	Nov. 17	Apr. 14
May 21	Oct. 16	Nov. 22	Apr. 19
May 26	Oct. 21	Nov. 27	Apr. 24
May 31	Oct. 26	Dec. 2	Apr. 29
Jun. 5	Oct. 31	Dec. 7	May 4
Jun. 10	Nov. 5	Dec. 12	May 9
Jun. 15	Nov. 10	Dec. 17	May 14
Jun. 20	Nov. 15	Dec. 22	May 19
Jun. 25	Nov. 20	Dec. 27	May 24

APPENDIX THREE

List of Tools, Equipment, and Sources

NATIONAL SHEEP-SUPPLY COMPANIES

Most everything you need for living with sheep can be purchased at your local farm-supply store. Buying locally benefits your local agricultural economy and keeps your shipping costs down. Unless you live in serious sheep country, however, your local shop will not stock sheep-specific vaccines and specialized tools. For that reason, and for price comparison purposes, here is the contact information for the major national sheep-supply companies that have Web sites.

Mid-States Livestock Supplies
125 East 10th Ave.
South Hutchinson, KS 67505
800-835-9665 or
9449 Basil-Western Rd. NW
Canal Winchester, OH 43110
800-841-9665
http://www.midstateswoolgrowers.com

Pipestone Veterinary Supply
1300 S. Hwy 75
P.O. Box 188
Pipestone, MN 56164
800-658-2523
http://www.pipevet.com

Premier 1
2031 300th St.
Washington, IA 52353
800-282-6631
http://www.premier1supplies.com

Sheepman Supply
8102 Liberty Road
Frederick, MD 21702
800-331-9122
http://www.sheepman.com

Sydell, Inc.
Rt. 1, Box 85
Burbank, SD 57010
800-842-1369
http://www.sydell.com

USEFUL PUBLICATIONS

Magazines
Subscribing to a magazine or two will bring you all sorts of good ideas, keep you up to date, and spark interesting conversations around your coffee table. Here are three good choices:

sheep! Subscriptions
W11564 Hwy. 64
Withee, WI 54498
715-785-7414

The Shepherd Magazine
Sheep and Farm Life, Inc.
5696 Johnston Road
New Washington, OR 44854-9736
419-492-2364

The Banner Sheep Magazine
P.O. Box 500
Cuba, IL 61427

Sheep Production Handbook
If you've already decided you want more information about any aspect of raising sheep, I recommend you buy the *Sheep Production Handbook* from the American Sheep Industry Association. This book (in 8.5" x 11" format) is more than 1,000 pages long, is often used as a textbook for college-level sheep-production courses, and has something on everything from grazing to genetics to predator control. The American Sheep Industry Association's Web site is pretty good too—and you can buy the book there.

American Sheep Industry Association
9785 Maroon Circle
Suite 360
Centennial, CO 80112
303-771-3500
www.sheepusa.org

TOOLS AND INFORMATION BY CHAPTER

Chapter 2: Choosing a Flock

Oklahoma State University maintains a wonderful Web site with the photographs and brief histories of nearly 300 varieties of sheep. If you're trying to decide on a breed, or merely want to be astonished at the wide range of colors and shapes that sheep come in, go to http://www.ansi.okstate.edu/breeds/sheep.

Chapter 3: Where Your Sheep Will Live

Portable shade canopy

These are best purchased locally—since their heavy weight can lead to hefty shipping charges—but try a Web search for "portable shade canopy" for comparison shopping. You won't need any sides, just poles, anchors, and a roof.

Building shelters

There are many wonderful books in print on how to build farm buildings. Try a Web search on "building a pole barn" to get started.

Shovel, pitchfork, and wheelbarrow

Any old set will do for cleaning manure and bedding out of the barn. If you aren't using a tractor or truck, consider a wheelbarrow as well.

Tractor

This is by no means required, but it sure is handy for moving manure, composting manure, and mowing pastures in the summer. It doesn't need to be fancy, and you can even borrow your neighbor's. Make sure it has a bucket loader in front!

Shavings and sawdust

Try a local sawmill or woodshop for free (or cheap) bulk quantities. Otherwise, buy compressed shavings by the bale at your local feed store. A bale goes a long way: one or two bales per sheep per winter ought to do it.

Mulch hay or straw

Mulch hay is any hay of low quality that you can buy on the cheap. Figure on $1 to $3 per bale. Straw is either grain stems that were cut before the seeds became viable or the leftover stems after the grain was winnowed. Figure on $4 to $8 per bale of straw. You can usually buy this through your local feed store or directly from a neighbor.

Lime

Any old agricultural lime will do. Figure on one fifty-pound bag per dozen sheep per winter.

Chapter 4: Feeding Your Sheep

Minerals

Visit your local feed store for either a solid block or a bag of powdered minerals. Make sure it's for sheep, not horses or cows; sheep need much less copper than other livestock.

Mineral feeder

Any old container will do as long as it keeps the minerals dry and the sheep can stick their noses into it. I use a shallow, plastic tray from the feed store that I've screwed to the inside wall of the shelter. Whatever you do, keep the feeder off the ground so that the animals won't step in it and muck it up.

Grain

Most feed stores sell a general-purpose sheep mix, which works for me. Check the label to make sure it isn't medicated and doesn't contain any animal protein. Special lamb mixes are also usually available for creep feeding.

Grain feeder

As with the mineral feeder, you want your grain feeder up off the ground by a foot or two. I use my hay feeder for grain, too, throwing in the grain on the bottom before piling the hay on top. Alternatively, you can make or buy a shallow tray and screw it to the shelter wall. Two details to keep in mind: make sure all the animals can access grain at the same time (so the biggest and strongest won't dominate the feeder) and arrange it so that you can fill the grain feeder from outside the pen (away from the serious jostling brought on by grain.)

Scale

A scale is nice for weighing grain, hay, and even baby lambs. Two good choices are a hanging spring scale, to which you can attach a tray (for grain) or canvas sling (for hay and lambs), or an old-style baby scale that sits on a table or flat surface. I bought an old baby scale at a yard sale and have been very happy with it.

Coffee can or scoop

You'll need some sort of can or scoop for dealing out grain and powdered minerals. Either way, once you figure out the proper quantities, mark the can or scoop for easy reference. The coffee cans I use are the large two-pound cans.

Hay

Tender second-cut hay is what you're after, and figure on $2 to $4 per forty-pound square bale. Having a few lesser quality bales on hand can also be good if your sheep start to score in the 4 range during the winter. You can always use these during weaning, too.

Hay feeder

A good hay feeder has two parts: a hay rack and a shelf underneath it. The rack holds the hay up where the sheep can pull it out as they need it. The shelf catches the loose stuff for later consumption and can also be used for grain. Use either metal panels (available from Premier 1) or wooden slats to make the hay rack, and position the rack close to vertical so that hay will only be dispensed when the animals pull on it. (Otherwise, hay will be wasted and get caught in the fleeces.) Also, try to set up the hay feeder so that you can fill the feeder from outside the pen without having to get your shoes mucky.

Premier 1 has a nice set of hay-feeder plans on their Web site. I made my own, roughly following their design and using their metal panels for the hay rack.

Whisk broom

Keeping your various feeders clean is an important part of having healthy sheep. I bought a small whisk broom from a hardware store and use it before each feeding to remove leftovers and debris.

Water buckets

Your sheep will drink roughly one-half to two gallons of water per animal per day. In the winter, when I'm feeding twice per day and water tends to freeze, I use small rubber pails (from the feed-supply store) and fill them just enough. In the summer, I have a larger, plastic tub that I fill for half a week at a time. In both cases, I try to set the water about a foot above the ground to keep the sheep from walking in it.

Auto waterers

Check your local store or one of the national sources if you want to try a higher tech solution.

Chapter 5: Fencing

Premier 1 puts out an excellent fencing catalog that describes both the various options and their rough cost per foot. Call them or visit their Web site for more details (the contact information is at the start of this appendix).

Charger

Buy a charger that uses high-voltage pulses as nearly all the newer chargers do, rather than continuous current. High-voltage pulses are less dangerous to humans, require less electricity, don't melt portable netting, and do a better job combating weeds. Solar-powered charges are commonly available these days and are a good solution if you don't have ready access to AC power. Because the solar kit costs a fair bit, however, I'd recommend using an AC model if it's at all convenient.

Grounding rods

Buy copper grounding rods at your local hardware store. You'll need at least three of these for grounding the charger and fence.

Lightning choke

I didn't install a lightning choke until after my first charger had been burnt to a crisp. Too bad: the choke costs $20, and the charger $200. Buy a lightning choke from a national supplier if your local store doesn't have one, and be sure to follow the directions exactly. When properly installed, the choke will prevent a nearby lightning strike from going through your fence and damaging the charger (and possibly your home's electrical supply).

High-tensile wire

Electric fence wire comes in long rolls that are both heavy to carry and difficult to manage. I strongly recommend that you make, buy, or rent some sort of spool dispenser to pay out the wire as you string it. It is nearly impossible otherwise to prevent the spool from "springing" out of your bare hands and turning into an impossible tangle.

Feed cable

You'll want at least a short length of shielded cable for running the electricity from the charger to the fence. This is also handy for running the charge underneath gates and anywhere else human hands are likely to be fumbling.

Testing meter

You can spend anywhere from $10 to $100 on a meter for testing whether or not your fence is shorted out somewhere. I have a small and relatively simple set of fences, and the cheap meter has been just fine for me.

Wooden gates

Wooden gates will give your operation a rustic, homespun feeling and can be made on the cheap using scrap lumber. Make the gate four feet tall or so, and either space the slats less than six inches apart or staple woven wire or other fencing to the wooden frame to prevent animals from escaping or getting their heads stuck.

Metal gates

I've used mostly dairy-cattle metal gates on our farm, since that's what our local store sells. I lash a section of woven wire to each gate to reduce the opening size sufficiently so it's safe for sheep. Metal gates designed for sheep can also be purchased from a national supplier, though the shipping can add up in a hurry.

Spring gates

Spring gates are sections of slinky-like coils that are strung across an opening to create a barrier. It's difficult to space the coils close enough together to be an effective barrier for sheep, but they are very convenient for diverting sheep from one pasture to another by opening or blocking laneways.

Woven wire gates

As I mentioned in the main text, if you have a place where you only need to open a gate once or twice a year or so, you can make a gate using just woven wire and posts. Drive a post on either side of your gateway, and lean a free post against one side. Run your wire fencing across the gateway and attach it to the free post. Then lash the free post to the fixed post, and you have your gate. It's not too convenient to open, but when you want to, simply unlash the free post and peel back the fencing to open the gate.

Moveable panels

Moveable panels can be very helpful for closing sheep into their confinement pen, creating a creep, or setting up lambing jugs. These are simply wooden gates or metal gates that are off their hinges for easy moving. Eight-foot panels are handy for two people to use, or two four-foot panels hinged together in the middle make nice lambing jugs.

Woven wire

Woven wire is the standard stuff used for non-electrified sheep fencing. Note that woven wire comes with various spacings between the vertical wires: three-inch is best for the barnyard, shelter area, confinement pen, and anywhere else that will confine young lambs; six-inch is cheaper and works fine for perimeter fencing and laneways that will guide but not contain the flock.

Fence posts
Fence posts come in two flavors—metal and wood. Metal posts are somewhat more expensive to buy, far easier to pound in, last for decades, and are less aesthetically pleasing (in my view) than wooden posts. Wooden posts are the opposite; even if they are cedar or other rot-resistant wood, they rarely last more than a decade or so, and as they become loose teeth near the ends of their lives, they make the fence very unreliable. I use mostly metal fence posts, with wooden posts reserved for the high visibility areas near the house. Both types should be easily purchased from your local supply store.

Fencing tool
One of the great joys of fencing is getting to use a bonafide fencing tool. These are perfect for holding staples, pulling staples, bending clips, bending wire, and cutting wire. Buy yourself one and paint it a bright color that will stand out when you drop it in the weeds somewhere.

Portable netting
Portable netting, in my view, is revolutionary. It looks so simple, yet it has been highly engineered to be lightweight, effective, and reasonably tangle-free. (Borrow an old roll from a friend to convince yourself that the current stuff is amazing.) There are two tricks to remember when handling netting. First, when paying it out, walk backward so your feet won't get tangled in the netting. Second, when picking it up, don't roll it. Instead, gather all the posts in one hand as you go, letting the netting hang down between them. When you have it all in hand, lay it on the ground and roll the netting up to the posts. This will prevent tangles next time you pay it out.

Chapter 7: Raising Your Own Lambs
Jugs
Either buy jug panels or make them out of wood (see "wooden panels" above).

Clean towels
Any old clean towels will work. Amniotic fluid is amazingly gooey, so figure on two towels per lamb.

Sharp scissors
If they aren't sharp, they won't be able to cut the umbilical cord cleanly.

Iodine and film canister
Any veterinary-grade iodine will do.

Lamb-saver gel
Buy the stuff in the convenient pump bottle, but make sure the pump stays vertical during the off-season. It will leak otherwise, and the oily, gooey stuff is impossible to clean up.

Molasses
If you're only talking a few ewes, household molasses is great. Otherwise, you can buy animal-grade molasses for cheap at the feed store. Add one cup of molasses per gallon of warm water.

Pencil and paper
For names, weights, and dates.

J-Jelly
As small a tube of this as you can buy will be fine. You'll hardly ever need it.

Disposable gloves
Any old latex or synthetic rubber glove will do. It's just nice to keep your hands clean sometimes, especially when putting iodine on umbilical cords.

Elbow-length disposable gloves
If you should need to extricate a tangled lamb inside its mom, these are a nice way to keep things sterile. Try one of the national suppliers for these.

Lambing snare
This can either be a specially designed piece of rubber (try one of the national suppliers) or a half-dozen lengths of string about two feet long each.

Powdered colostrum

If you have a bottle lamb, you'll need to feed powdered colostrum first. A small package makes a lot and can be stored for a long period, provided you seal the package up after use.

Powdered replacement milk

You might even wait until you actually have a bottle lamb to buy this, since you can feed powdered colostrum for the first few days. Figure on one small bag per lamb per year.

Jug feeders for hay, grain, and water

These containers don't have to be anything special, but they do need to be tall enough to prevent the lambs from gaining access and prevent spillage. We live in the maple-sugaring belt, so I use old sap buckets, which are narrow and tall. But most anything will work, including five-gallon plastic buckets.

Open container for placenta

Something with high sides and no holes in the bottom is great. I use an old plastic flower pot. Layer in some hay to absorb moisture.

Elastrator and bands

You'll probably need to try one of the national supply stores for these, and there's no homemade substitute that will work.

Ear tags and applicator

Try a national supply store if your local shop only sells large tags for horses and cows. Make sure that you have the right applicator tool for the tags you're using. For only a few extra bucks, the national stores will even print your farm name right on each tag.

Creep and creep feeder

Use any old panels or wood to create the creep and a feeder for grain. The key is the doorway. You can either buy specially designed, adjustable creep doors from one of the national stores, or you can make your own out of wood, attaching the wood using drywall screws so that it's easy to adjust the size to be just right for your lambs.

Bottle and nipples

Either use a baby bottle, in which case you'll want to slightly enlarge the hole in the nipple, or buy lamb nipples that can be attached to soda bottles.

Chapter 8: Shearing and Wool

Extension cord

The electric shears use a fair bit of juice, so make sure you have a heavy gauge, grounded cord—not a two-wire lamp cord from the house.

Clean tarp or plywood sheet

Most anything will do for this so long as it's clean.

Skirting table

This can be as simple or as fancy as you like. I use the four-foot by eight-foot sheet of plywood that the shearer stands on and put it on sawhorses. Or you can build a slatted table. Anything that gets the wool up off the floor will work.

Old bedsheets

Bedsheets are great for gathering up fleeces as they are removed from the sheep. They're large and porous enough to allow the wool to cool without molding.

Fleece bags

If you run out of bedsheets, store your wool in breathable bags—either specially designed fleece bags or any burlap or non-synthetic bag. Plastic trash bags are OK in the short term but are likely to cause molding in the long term. Plastic feedbags are out because any stray plastic fibers from the bag will contaminate the fleece.

Broom

Have a broom on hand for sweeping up the belly wool and anything else you don't want added to the fleeces.

Chapter 9: The Health of Your Sheep

Hoof trimmers or knife

A good set of hand pruning shears can get you started in the hoof trimming business, or you can buy special hoof shears. I've also watched our vet wield a hoof knife to good effect, though the knife requires a good deal more skill than the shears.

De-wormers

Buy these from a national supplier if your local shop doesn't stock them. In order to prevent your sheep from developing resistance to de-wormers, be sure to always use the full dose, minimize the number of times you use de-wormer, and use more than one type during the year. For example, I use Panacur paste in the spring and Ivermec drench in the summer and fall. Most de-wormers last for several years without refrigeration.

Drenching syringe

The best drenching syringes have metal tubes; they cost a few more bucks, but they last forever. My sheep usually chew on the tube as I'm drenching them, which will destroy a plastic syringe in no time at all.

Needles and syringes

The general rule is twenty-gauge, half-inch needles for subcutaneous and eighteen-gauge, one-inch needles for intramuscular. Don't reuse needles, because they dull quickly and can cross contaminate either the sheep or the medicine vial.

CD/T

Ewes need a CD/T injection once per year, lambs twice. The vaccine stores for up to three years in the refrigerator, so you can buy a reasonable amount at one time.

Pepto-Bismol

Sometimes sheep get the runs, especially during times of dietary transition. A day or two of liquid pink can be just the thing to fix what ails them. Dose them just as you do people; if that doesn't work after two days, call the vet.

Chapter 10: Slaughter and Butchering

Panels and fencing

See the fencing section above: a few of these panels are key for separating and corralling your animals if the slaughter is happening at your place.

Head harness

You can buy a head harness for controlling a sheep while moving it around in the open, such as between your confinement pen and your truck. It's almost impossible to pull a sheep along using such a contraption, however, so I use it more as insurance: we can grab the rope as as animal escapes but don't use it as a leash.

Waiver and list of customers

Your butcher may require your customers to sign a waiver if the meat is not USDA inspected, so find this out in advance.

Freezer

One lamb, butchered and returned to you in butcher paper, will fill up between 1.5 to 2 brown paper shopping bags worth of space. Make sure you have it! If you are planning to have your customers come to your place to collect their meat, make sure they can come right away (unless you have sufficient freezer space for everything).

Cooperative Extension Offices

ALABAMA
Auburn University
Extension Youth Animal
    Science
Robert A. Ebert
209 Animal Sciences
Auburn, AL 36849-5625
334-844-1563
www.aces.edu

ALASKA
University of Alaska
    Fairbanks
Extension Sheep Specialist
Milan Shipka
P.O Box 756180
Fairbanks, AK 99775
907-474-7188
www.uaf.edu/ces

ARIZONA
University of Arizona
Extension Livestock
    Specialist
Robert M. Kattnig
Animal Science Department
239 Shantz Building
Tucson, AZ 85721
602-621-9757
www.ag.arizona.edu/
    extension

ARKANSAS
University of Arkansas
Extension Livestock Specialist
Tom R. Troxel
2301 S. University Avenue
P.O. Box 391
Little Rock, AR 72203-0391
501-671-2188
Fax: 501-671-2185
www.uaex.edu

CALIFORNIA
University of California
Extension Animal
    Management Systems
    Specialist
James Oltjen
Animal Science Department
Davis, CA 95616-8521
530-752-5650
Fax: 530-752-0175
http://ucanr.org/ces/cea.shtml

COLORADO
Colorado State University
Extension Sheep/Wool
    Specialist
Steve LeValley
105 B Animal Science
Ft. Collins, CO 80524
970-491-1321
Fax: 970-491-5326
www.ext.colostate.edu

CONNECTICUT
University of Connecticut
Extension Sheep Specialist
Thomas Hoagland
U-40 Dept. of Animal Science
Storrs, CT 06269-4040
860-486-1069
Fax: 860-486-4375
www.canr.uconn.edu/ces

DELAWARE
University of Delaware
Extension Livestock
    Specialist
Limin Kung Jr.
Animal/Food Science Dept.
33 Townsend Hall
Newark, DE 19716
302-831-2522
Fax: 302-831-2822
http://ag.udel.edu/extension

FLORIDA
University of Florida
Extension Livestock Specialist
Saundra Tenbroeck
C 231 Animal Science Bldg.
Gainesville, FL 32611
352-392-2789
Fax: 352-392-7652
http://edis.ifas.ufl.edu

GEORGIA
University of Georgia
Extension Animal Scientist
Timothy Wilson
East GA Extension Center
P.O. Box 8112
Statesboro, GA 30460
912-681-5639
http://extension.caes.uga.edu

HAWAII
University of Hawaii
Extension Livestock
   Specialist
Brent Buckley
Animal Science Dept.
1955 E. West Road
Honolulu, HI 96822-2318
808-956-7090
Fax: 808-956-4883
www2.ctahr.hawaii.edu/
   extout/extout.asp

IDAHO
University of Idaho
Extension Sheep Specialist
Caine Vet Teaching and
   Research Center
1020 E. Homedale Road
Caldwell, ID 83605
208-454-8657
www.uidaho.edu/ag/
   extension

ILLINOIS
University of Illinois
Extension Sheep Specialist
Alan R. Cobb
128 ASL MC-630
1207 W Gregory
Urbana, IL 61801
217-333-7351
Fax: 217-244-3169
www.extension.uiuc.edu

INDIANA
Purdue University
Extension Sheep Specialist
Michael Neary
Animal Science Department
1151 Lilly Hall
West Lafayette, IN 47906
765-494-4849
www.ces.purdue.edu

IOWA
Iowa State University
Extension Sheep Specialist
Daniel G. Morrical
Animal Science Dept.
337 Kildee Hall
Ames, IA 50011-3150
515-294-2904
www.extension.iastate.edu

KANSAS
Kansas State University
Extension Sheep Specialist
Clifford W. Spaeth
228 Weber Hall
Manhattan, KS 66506-0201
785-532-1255
www.o2net.ksu.edu

KENTUCKY
University of Kentucky
Extension Sheep Specialist
Guy L.M. Chappell
Animal Science Department
911 W.P. Garrigus Bldg. 0215
Lexington, KY 40546-0215
606-257-2716
www.ca.uky.edu/ces

LOUISIANA
Louisiana State University
Extension Sheep Specialist
Terry Dumas
Agricultural Center
P.O. Box 25058
Baton Rouge, LA 70894-5058
225-578-2412
www.lsuagcenter.com/nav/
   extension/extension.asp

MAINE
University of Maine
Extension Livestock
   Specialist
Kenneth Andries
5735 Hitchner Hall
Orono, ME 04469-5735
207-581-2789
www.umext.edu

MARYLAND
University of Maryland
Extension Sheep Specialist
Susan G. Schoenian
AGNR- MCE- Region 1
NA Salisbury
College Park, MD 20742-5515
410-749-6141
www.agnr.umd.edu/mce

MASSACHUSETTS
University of Massachusetts
Extension Sheep Specialist
Mark T. Huyler
302 Stockbridge Hall
Amherst, MA 01003
413-545-2344
www.umassextension.org

MICHIGAN
Michigan State University
Extension Sheep Specialist
Margaret Benson
Dept. of Animal Science
2265 K Anthony Hall
East Lansing, MI 48824
517-432-1388
www.msue.msu.edu/home/

MINNESOTA
University of Minnesota
Extension Sheep Specialist
William Head
West Central Research &
   Outreach Center
46352 State Hwy 329
P.O. Box 471
Morris, MN 56267-04/1
320-598-1711
www.extension.umn.edu

MISSISSIPPI
Mississippi State University
Extension Sheep Specialist
Michael E. Boyd
Animal Science Dept.
P.O. Box 9815
Mississippi State, MS 39762-
9815
601-325-2802
http://msucares.com

MISSOURI
University of Missouri
Livestock Specialist
James R. Humphrey
University Extension Center
P.O. Box 32
Savannah, MO 64485
816-324-3147
http://muextension.
missouri.edu

MONTANA
Montana State University
Extension Sheep Specialist
Rodney Kott
Animal/Range Sciences Dept.
221 Linfield Hall
Bozeman, MT 59717-2820
406-994-3415
www.msu.montana.edu

NEBRASKA
University of Nebraska
Extension Livestock
    Management Specialist
Bryan A. Reiling
Animal Science Dept.
Room C204
Lincoln, NE 68583-0908
402-472-8960
www.extension.unl.edu

NEVADA
University of Nevada - Reno
Extension Sheep Specialist
Hudson Glimp
Mail Stop 202
FA 225A
Reno, NV 89557-0104
775-784-4254
www.unce.unr.edu

NEW HAMPSHIRE
University of New
    Hampshire
Extension Sheep Specialist
Bruce Clement
Co-op Extension
800 Park Avenue
Keene, NH 03431-1513
603-862-2033
http://ceinfo.unh.edu

NEW JERSEY
Rutgers, The State University
    of New Jersey
Extension Sheep Specialist
Michael Westendorf
Animal Science Dept.
84 Lipman Drive
New Brunswick, NJ 08901-
8525
732-932-9408
www.rce.rutgers.edu

NEW MEXICO
New Mexico State University
Extension Sheep Specialist
Clay Mathis
MSC 3AE, Box 30003
Las Cruces, NM 88003-8001
505-646-8022
www.cahe.nmsu.edu/ces

NEW YORK
Cornell University
Extension Sheep Specialist
Michael L. Thonney
114 Morrison Hall
Ithaca, NY 14853-4801
607-255-2851
www.cce.cornell.edu

NORTH CAROLINA
North Carolina State
    University
Extension Livestock
    Specialist
Matthew Poore
105 B Polk Hall
P.O. Box 7621
Raleigh, NC 27695-7621
919-515-7798
www.ces.ncsu.edu

NORTH DAKOTA
North Dakota State
    University
Extension Sheep Specialist
Roger Haugen
100-E Hultz Hall
Fargo, ND 58105-5053
701-231-7645
www.ext.nodak.edu

OHIO
The Ohio State University
Extension Sheep Specialist
Roger A. High
Dept. of Animal Sciences
2029 Fyffe Rd
Animal Science Bldg, Rm 222 E
Columbus, OH 43210
614-292-0589
http://extension.osu.edu

OKLAHOMA
Oklahoma State University
Extension Sheep Specialist
Gerald Fitch
Animal Science Department
109 Animal Science Bldg.
Stillwater, OK 74078-6051
405-744-6065
www1.dasnr.okstate.edu/oecs

OREGON
Oregon State University
Extension Sheep Specialist
James Thompson
Animal Science Dept.
112 Withycombe Hall
Corvallis, OR 97331-6702
541-737-1908
http://extension.oregonstate.
    edu

PENNSYLVANIA
Pennsylvania State University
Extension Sheep Contact
Keith Bryan
0317 Henning Building
University Park, PA 16802
814-863-0569
www.extension.psu.edu

RHODE ISLAND
University of Rhode Island
Extension Sheep Specialist
Katherine H. Petersson
Fisheries/Animal/
    Vet Science Dept.
20 B Woodward Hall
Kingston, RI 02881-0804
401-874-2951
www.uri.edu/cc

SOUTH CAROLINA
Clemson University
Extension Sheep Specialist
Harold D. Hupp
Animal & Veterinary Science
140 Poole Ag Center
Clemson, SC 29634
803-656-5161
www.clemson.edu/extension

SOUTH DAKOTA
South Dakota State
    University
Extension Sheep Specialist
Jeff Held
ASC 0112/2170
Brookings, SD 57007
605-688-5433
http://sdces.sdstate.edu

TENNESSEE
University of Tennessee
Extension Sheep Specialist
Warren Gill
Animal Science
5201 Marchant Drive
Nashville, TN 37211-5112
615-832-8341
www.utextension.utk.edu

TEXAS
Texas A & M University
Extension Sheep Specialist
B. Frank Craddock
7887 US Highway 87 North
San Angelo, TX 76901-9714
915-653-4576
http://texasextension.tamu.edu

UTAH
Utah State University
Extension Sheep Specialist
C. Kim Chapman
250 North Main St.
Richfield, UT 84701-2165
435-893-0474
http://extension.usu.edu

VERMONT
University of Vermont
Extension Sheep Specialist
Chester (Chet) Parsons
Animal Science Department
Burlington, VT 05405
802-524-6501
www.uvm.edu/~uvmext/

VIRGINIA
Virginia Technological
    University
Extension Sheep Specialist
Scott Greiner
Animal/Poultry Science Dept.
Blacksburg, VA 24061-0306
540-23 1-9 159
www.ext.vt.edu

WASHINGTON
Washington State University
Extension Sheep Specialist
Jan Busboom
Animal Science Dept.
Clark 123
Pullman, WA 99164-6310
509-335-2880
http://ext.wsu.edu

WISCONSIN
University of Wisconsin
Extension Sheep Specialist
Dave Thomas
438 Animal Science Bldg.
1675 Observatory Drive
Madison, WI 53706
608-263-4306
www.uwex.edu/ces

WEST VIRGINIA
West Virginia University
Extension Sheep Specialist
Deborah J. Marsh
P.O. Box 96
Franklin, WV 26807
304-358-3660
www.wvu.edu/~exten/

WYOMING
University of Wyoming
Extension Sheep Specialist
Robert H. Stobart
Animal Science Dept.
Agriculture C405
Laramie, WY 82071
307-766-5212
www.uwyo.edu/ces/
    ceshome.htm

APPENDIX FIVE

Breed Associations

American Black Sheep Registry
4714 North Glade Road
Loveland, CO 80538-9528

American Livestock Breeds Conservancy
P.O. Box 477
Pittsboro, NC 27312
www.albc-usa.org

Barbados Blackbelly Sheep Association International
552 NE 100th Lane
Lamar, MO 64759
www.blackbellysheep.org

Black Welsh Mountain Sheep Association
P.O. Box 534
Paonia, CO 81428-0534
www.blackwelsh.org

Bluefaced Leicester Union of North America
769 W. "VW" Ave
Schoolcraft, MI 49087-9752

Border Leicester Association
P.O. Box 947
Canby, OR 97013-0947
www.ablasheep.org

California Red Sheep Registry
1850 Reilly Road
Merced, CA 95340-8958
www.cell2000.net/
ca_redsheep.com

Cheviot Sheep Society
RR1 Box 120
New Richland, MN 56072

Clun Forest Association
21727 Randall Drive
Houston, MN 55943
www.clunforestsheep.org

Columbia Sheep Breeders Association
2821 State Hwy 182
Nevada, OH 44849
www.columbiasheep.org

Coopworth Sheep Society of North America
25101 Chris Lane NE
Kingston, WA 98346-9303

Cormo Sheep Association
HC 59, Box 5925
Broadus, MT 59317-9803

Corriedale Association
P.O. Box 391
Clay City, IL 62824-0391
www.americancorriedale.com

Cotswold Breeders Association
5223 Hanover Pike
Manchester, MD 21102

Debouillet Sheep Breeders Association
P.O. Box 67
Picacho, NM 88343

Delaine-Merino Record Association
15603-173rd Ave.
Milo, IA 50166
www.admra.org

Dorper Sheep Breeders Society
1120 Wilkes Blvd.
Columbia, MO 65201
www.dorperamerica.org

Dorset Club
P.O. Box 506
N. Scituate, RI 02857-0506
www.dorsets.homestead.com

East Friesian Sheep contact
www.finnsheep.asn.au

Finnsheep Breeders' Association
HC65 Box 517
Hominy, OK 74035
www.finnsheep.org/

Gulf Coast Sheep Breeders Association
2262 Highway 59
Spruce Pine, AL 35585

Hampshire Sheep Association
15603-173rd Avenue
Milo, IA 50166-9667
www.countrylovin.com/ahsa/
index.html

Icelandic Sheep Breeders of North America
115772 Hwy. 395
Topaz, CA 96133
www.isbona.com

Jacob Sheep Breeders Association
P.O. Box 10472
Bozeman, MT 59719
www.jsba.org

Karakul Sheep Registry
11500 Hwy 5
Boonville, MO 65233
www.karakulsheep.com

**Katahdin Hair Sheep
  International**
P.O. Box 778B
Fayetteville, AR 72702
www.khsi.org

**Lincoln Sheep Breeders
  Association**
15603 173rd Ave.
Milo, IA 50166
www.lincolnsheep.org

**Montadale Sheep Breeders
  Association**
2514 Willow Road, NE
Fargo, ND 58102
www.montadales.com

**Natural Colored Wool
  Growers Association**
429 West U.S. 30
Valparaiso, IN 46385

**Navajo-Churro Sheep
  Association**
P.O. Box 94
Ojo Caliente, NM 87549-0094
www.navajo-churrosheep.com

**North Country Cheviot
  Sheep Association**
8708 S. CR 500 W.
Reelsville, IN 46171

Oxford Sheep Association
1960 East 2100 North Road
Stonington, IL 62567-5338

Panama Sheep Breed contact
University of Idaho
AVS Dept
Moscow, ID 83843

**Perendale Sheep
  Association**
18811 New Hampshire Ave.
Ashton, MD 20861

Polypay Sheep Association
15603-173rd Ave.
Milo, IA 50166

**Rambouillet Sheep
  Breeders Association**
1610 South State Road 3261
Levelland, TX 79336-9230
www.rambouilletsheep.org

**Romanov Sheep
  Association**
P.O. Box 1126
Pataskala, OH 43062-1126

**Romney Breeders
  Association**
744 Riverbanks Road
Grants Pass, OR 97527-9607
www.americanromney.org

**Scottish Blackface Sheep
  Breeders Association**
Windfall Farms
1699 H H Highway
Willow Springs, MO 65793-
9204

**Shetland Sheep Breeders
  Association**
2400 Faussett Road
Howell, MI 48843
www.shetland-sheep.org

**Shropshire Registry
  Association**
P.O. Box 635
Harvard, IL 60033-0635
www.shropshires.org

**Southdown Breeders
  Association**
HCR 13 Box 220
Fredonia, TX 76842-9702
www.southdownsheep.org

**St. Croix Hair Sheep
  International**
15603 173rd Ave.
Milo, IA 50166
www.stcroixsheep.org

Suffolk Sheep Association
17 West Main
P.O. Box 256
Newton, UT 84327-0256
www.u-s-s-a.org

Targhee Sheep Association
P.O. Box 427
Chinook, MT 59523

**Texel Sheep Breeders'
  Society**
P.O. Box 86
Broadus, MY 59317
www.usatexels.org

Tunis Sheep Registry Inc.
819 Lyons Street
Ludlow, MA 01056
www.tunissheep.org

**Wensleydale Sheep
  Association**
4589 Fruitland Road
Loma Rica, CA 95901-8706
www.wensleydalesheep.org

Wiltshire Horn
American Livestock Breeds
  Conservancy
Box 477
Pittsboro, NC 27312
http://www.albc-usa.org

INDEX